THE VILLAGE IN THE JUNGLE

LEONARD WOOLF was born in London in 1880. The first landmark in his career was undoubtedly Cambridge and the friends he made there. The next was Ceylon, where he served in the Civil Service from 1904 to 1911. He was Assistant Government Agent in Hambantota – the 'Kamburupitiya' of *The Village in the Jungle* – when he went to England on leave.

In 1912 he resigned from the colonial service to marry Virginia Stephen, the writer.

He made a new career for himself in the world of letters and politics in London as writer, editor and journalist. In 1917 with his wife, Virginia Woolf, he founded one of the most individual and successful publishing firms, The Hogarth Press. For many years he took an active part in politics and the activities of the Labour Party. He began writing his *Autobiography* when he was nearly eighty and it will be by that work as well as *The Village in the Jungle* that he will be best remembered as a writer. Leonard Woolf died in 1969, aged eighty-nine.

E.F.C. LUDOWYK was born in Ceylon in 1906 and was educated there at mission school and at University College, Colombo. He spent three years at Cambridge – from 1929 to 1932 – and then returned to Colombo, where he was subsequently Professor of English at the University from 1936 until his retirement in 1956. His books include *The Footprint of the Buddha* (1958), *The Modern History of Ceylon* (1966), *The Story of Ceylon* (1962) and *Understanding Shakespeare* (1962).

LEONARD WOOLF

The Village in the Jungle

WITH AN INTRODUCTION BY
E.F.C. LUDOWYK

Oxford   New York   Toronto   Delhi
OXFORD UNIVERSITY PRESS
1981

Oxford University Press, Walton Street, Oxford OX2 6DP

London Glasgow New York Toronto
Delhi Bombay Calcutta Madras Karachi
Kuala Lumpur Singapore Hong Kong Tokyo
Nairobi Dar es Salaam Cape Town
Melbourne Auckland
and associate companies in
Beirut Berlin Ibadan Mexico City

Copyright M.T. Parsons 1913
Introduction © Oxford University Press 1981

First published by Edward Arnold Limited 1913

First Hogarth Press edition 1931
First issued as an Oxford University Press paperback 1981

British Library Cataloguing in Publication Data

Woolf, Leonard
The village in the jungle. – (Oxford paperbacks)
I. Title
823'.912(F) PR604.5.068
ISBN 0-19-281312-9

Printed in Great Britain by
Richard Clay (The Chaucer Press) Ltd
Bungay, Suffolk

To V. W.

I've given you all the little, that I've to give;
    You've given me all, that for me is all there is;
So now I just give back what you have given –
    If there is anything to give in this.

INTRODUCTION

BY E. F. C. LUDOWYK

LEONARD WOOLF was born in London, into a well-to-do
Jewish family, in 1880. His years at Cambridge were an
important formative period in his life, mainly on account of the
friendships he made there – with Lytton Strachey, E. M. Forster
and J. M. Keynes, among others. Fresh from university he went
out to Ceylon in 1904 as a cadet in the Ceylon Civil Service – the
small group of white administrators who ruled the island.

His intelligence and abilities attracted the attention of the
formidable Sir Hugh Clifford, the Colonial Secretary. So at the
early age of 28 Leonard Woolf found himself Assistant Government Agent – the chief administrative and judicial officer – at
Hambantota. He was responsible for an area as large as
Northamptonshire, sparsely populated, most of it in malarial
jungle in the dry zone of South Ceylon. He spent close upon
three years there, walking and riding his pony and his bicycle all
over the district.

He threw himself with energy into dealing with the problems
facing him as administrator – chiefly those of rural indebtedness
and rinderpest. He got to know the jungle very well, under the
tutelage of Engelbrecht, a Boer prisoner of war who preferred to
stay on in Ceylon after his period of internment there. He must
have realized, like all those who know the jungle, that, in the
words of a later German specialist on animals in East Africa,
'wild animals are more gentlemanly in their behaviour than
human beings'; yet he never overcame his feeling that the jungle
was 'cruel'.

He left Ceylon on leave in 1911, but decided to retire from the
colonial service in 1912. In the same year he married Virginia
Stephen, the sister of one of his Cambridge friends, and took up,
with the energy and enthusiasm which had marked his years in

Ceylon, the task of making a new career for himself in England.

He was talented, with a quick and receptive mind. He wrote easily and well and had views, at the time advanced, on such subjects as British colonial policy. Besides, he knew a number of people then beginning to make their mark in the worlds of literature and journalism. *The Village in the Jungle*, an imaginative record of another formative influence in his life – the years in Hambantota – was published in 1913 and reprinted twice in that year. It was dedicated to his wife, Virginia Woolf.

Leonard Woolf was connected with a number of enlightened and liberal causes during the 1914–18 war and after, more particularly with the preliminaries leading to the projected League of Nations. He was also, as he described himself later, 'a practical politician working in the Labour Party'. He wrote a number of books on socio-political subjects and worked prodigiously hard as essayist, reviewer and editor.

In 1917, together with his wife, whose career as a novelist had already begun, he founded The Hogarth Press. It soon developed into a successful and distinguished publishing house. As he stated later in his *Autobiography*, he took particular pride in the part this publishing house played in making the work of Freud available to the English reader.

Lowes Dickinson, in a letter to Leonard Woolf in the twenties, commented that 'this damned state of Europe keeps my nose on a peculiarly unpleasant grindstone, and the only result is that one's nose wears out and the grindstone doesn't'. If Leonard Woolf had had similar feelings about his own political writing, he could have had nothing but satisfaction and pleasure in the reception given to his *Autobiography*, which he began when he was nearly eighty. The five volumes were highly acclaimed. It is significant that, looking back over various stages in his life, he saw them as a plunge into the hazards of one jungle after another. They are an eminently readable and interesting record of persons and events in a long and crowded life, full of witty and sharp observation of human character and the practical business of making a living as a writer and publisher.

Leonard Woolf's friend from the Bloomsbury group, E. M.

Forster, once remarked that his 'lawgivers' were 'Erasmus and Montaigne'; Leonard Woolf would certainly have claimed Voltaire as one of his, for he took the ninety volumes of the latter's collected works with him to Ceylon.

He led a very active life, much involved with publishing and with his wife's work and her state of health until her death in 1941. He visited Ceylon briefly in 1960 and spoke with quiet satisfaction and some surprise at the warmth of the welcome he received, and even the fact that he was still remembered there.

Behind his novel, *The Village in the Jungle*, lie the antithetical suggestions of its title. To a European writing in the early years of this century the 'nature' of the jungle was naturally post-Darwinian. To Woolf, 'Nature' is neither 'heartless' nor 'neutral', as contemporary poets had suggested, but, in an earlier poetic phrase, 'red in tooth and claw' – the arena of the struggle for survival. He adds a moral judgement to this: the jungle is 'evil'.

Unfortunately this indictment runs counter to the real nature of the jungle as both the jungle-dweller and the white Hamadoru, who is a hunter, know it. Between Silindu and the animals there exists an understanding and humane relationship. He knows, as he talks to them in the language of folk tale, that they – like him – have to live.

Insistence on the 'evil' of the jungle in the opening of the novel appears forced, produced by constant repetition of the term, further touches being either repetitious, as, for instance, the use of 'slinking' (no fewer than six times in a few pages) to suggest furtive and sinister movement, or tired, like 'obscene' used of the cactus, to evoke savage, sacrilegious rites. The effect is as artfully contrived as Hardy's Egdon Heath.

At one of the novel's three climactic moments – the first of the three 'trials' – the jungle is placed in the totality of the writer's scheme: the wide vista from the courthouse, with sea, air and the jungle in the distance. This is more or less repeated, with one important difference, a few pages later. The court house, where the human action develops, 'seems very small now, suspended over this vast and soundless world of water and trees.'

The effect is paradoxical, both distancing the jungle and holding it closer. The panoramic view diminishes the human, yet the vast amphitheatre concentrates attention on the human action, elevating it in the foreground of one's vision. The long view is followed by the cutback, focusing on the dramatic moment. The jungle is neither character nor destiny; it is the envelope of the human action.

How then does 'evil' come into it? Devils are another matter. They are perfectly well known in Ceylon, but the jungle is not their preserve; besides there are conventional methods of dealing with them. They are too commonplace to be associated with 'evil'.

As for 'village', all its humane connotations are at odds with the comment that 'They [the people in the village] are very near to the animals which live in the jungle around them'. This statement, except for the significance of 'buffalo', as applied to Silindu, which will be taken up later, repudiates the total impression of the love subsisting between Silindu and his daughters, their feeling for their home and their rare human qualities.

Once again, at a crucial 'trial' – the enquiry in the judge's bungalow – attention is focused on the significance of a vital element in the novel. When the judge asks the Ratemahatmaya: 'Let's have your opinion of the chap here. He's a human being isn't he?', the latter's hesitant answer 'They kill like – like – animals, like the leopard, sir', is countered by the judge's: 'Savages, you mean. Well, I don't know. I rather doubt it.' The simple terms of this exchange are heightened by the irony in the judge's remark: 'I see you would make a very good judge, Ratemahatmaya.' A moment later he adds: 'They [the animals] won't touch you if you leave them alone.'

The exotic in both worlds – jungle and village – is important, but not fundamentally so. Humanity in general is the real subject here.

The story sets out in the traditional mode with the words 'In Beddagama there lived a man called Silindu...' The lucidity of the prose, the writer's ear for the locutions and rhythms of the

villagers' speech, the irony and the imagery which often sharpens
the point of a situation, reflect the controlling intelligence at
work behind the story.

The main character, Silindu (his toughness belies the soft and
mild connotations of his name*) and his family are all ordinary
inhabitants of a village presided over by a trinity of corrupt
official, medical practitioner and dealer in spells, and money-
lending trader. Exploited by all three, the villagers are unbeliev-
ably destitute, but the lives of those like Silindu's family are
enriched by a strong sense of attachment to their home and their
affection for each other. Behind them stands a culture of legend,
story and folk tale which gives their existence some meaning.

Silindu's family group is unusual in the fact that all its
members are rejects. Silindu is set apart from everybody by the
label *tikak pissu* — a blanket term which covers most things from
harmless eccentricity to dangerous unpredictability. His daughters have been brought up with a better knowledge of the jungle
than of their conventional duties. The relations of the family
with the rest of the village are not just stated; they are shown.
Nanchohami's outburst when Babun (the name, not unusual
then, is the Sinhalese transliteration of the Hindi honorific
'Baboo') declares his intention of marrying Punchi Menika,
registers the low degree of Silindu's family. It is presented as an
operatic aria: 'Nanchohami threw up her hands, and began in a
voice which shrilled and fluted with anger...' Hers is really a
virtuoso performance by an ageing prima donna.

The novel's structure emerges as a series of situations in which
reject becomes rebel, instrument becomes agent and passive
active. The character, becoming conscious of its real situation
and realizing the consequences of the courses open to it, makes a
responsible choice. This, as the story develops, leads to the
'trials' which decide the fate of the agent.

The situations arise out of three stories, all of them related to
the main character, Silindu. He is not the agent in any of them,
but is caught up in the toils of all three, until he sees and

* I owe this and various other points to discussion with the Ven. Bhikkhu W.
Rahula.

understands their origin. From being reject and passive, he, too, becomes rebel and agent.

The three stories — of Babun and Punchi Menika, of Punchirala and Hinnihami, and of Punchi Menika, Babun and Fernando — are similar and different. All of them originate in desire or craving.

The desire of Babun for Punchi Menika is natural, the shared and reciprocated love of two persons for each other. That of Punchirala and of Fernando is one person's abnormal passion to use another as a sexual object. As lust it is destructive.

Babun's love for Punchi Menika and her acceptance of him as her husband makes both of them rebels against their family and village opinion. They make their choice as free agents. It brings both, however briefly, a period of happiness. To Silindu, however, their marriage 'was only one more of the evils which inevitably came upon him'.

The second is the most dramatic and moving of the three stories, with its resonances of myth: the daughter who, to save her father's life, sacrifices herself to a malignant magician, escaping from his clutches only to perish later.

The story has, at times, all the magic of folk tale. 'But on the evening of the first day's journey, the one-eyed man will meet you in an open stony place beside two palu trees. Then you must go to him and say, "There is the girl; take her." He will take the girl, and the devil will leave the man.' And so it turned out.

Of all the rejects Hinnihami has most of the rebel in her. She reacts violently against the vederala, scorning his proposals 'with fury', as she is physically repelled by him. Yet she is powerless when Punchirala's machinations bring Silindu close to death.

After the trance-like experience of the pilgrimage to Beragama, with the excitement of the procession, she gives in.

Yet she struggles free, deliberately flouting the vederala, claiming with arrogance to be a yakkini. On her own she repudiates the decision made by her family to accept the command of the god to the holy man and leaves the vederala. As free agent she is a heroic figure: 'Are you frightened, Punchirala?

The binder of yakkas is frightened of the yakkini. You can tell her, they say, because her eyes are red and unblinking, and because she neither fears nor loves. It is better for you that I should go – to the trees from which I come, mighty vederala. Otherwise, I would strangle you, and eat you in the house.'

She is defeated, not by devils, nor by 'evil', but by the malignity of human beings – 'man's inhumanity to man'.

Throughout the episode the artist's dramatic skill in the handling of his material and his identification with the girl are abundantly clear.

The third story – of Fernando's attempt to seduce Punchi Menika – may seem a replay of an earlier reel. But there is a difference. This time the magic spell is money, in which Fernando is a passionate believer. With the great symbol of authority in the village, the headman, behind him, he sets out to get possession of the girl and the tacit connivance of her husband. His crude mode of attack and the stories he tells of 'rupees, bracelets, and anklets, and silk cloths' reflect the nastiness of the common crook. Rebuffed by both the girl and Babun, the conspirators institute false charges against the latter and Silindu, and the trial in the courthouse follows.

Only after his arrest does Silindu recognize what he had not perceived until then – the malignity of the headman. The long series of misfortunes he realizes, as Hinnihami had done, is due to human agents. 'To be hunted for years now and not to know it!'

After the trial when 'the white Hamadoru' has set him free and sentenced Babun to six months' rigorous imprisonment, Silindu accepts responsibility for his actions. The reject becomes a rebel. With deliberate irony he accepts the badge of 'stupid buffalo' fastened on him and turns tables on his hunters. The headman is cunningly lured away from Fernando and shot, and then Silindu blazes away with his muzzle-loader at all he can see of the sensualist – 'his fat stomach and legs'.

He decides to give himself up to official authority. At least 'the white Hamadoru' had understood and at the courthouse had asked him 'to go'. The three in the well lit room in the judge's bungalow compose a picture of imperialism in miniature: the white ruler in evening-dress sitting at his table; the 'bare-forked animal' squatting on the floor; the factor standing dutifully by. It should be noted, however, that the only sympathy shown Silindu in his plight has come from 'the white Hamadoru'. All he has received from the Ratemahatmaya has been kicks in the ribs. None the less the picture is a true likeness.

What follows in the room is the judge's descant on the theme of political science, suitably attuned to the level of the Ratemahatmaya's powers of comprehension. What is man and how should he be governed? The judge is as much the prisoner of the processes of law as are Silindu and Babun in their cage at the courthouse. It would, perhaps, have been better to have imprisoned Silindu too. Wouldn't it have been better not to stir the water, to let well alone? With fine irony, Woolf describes Silindu, the cause and subject of all these speculations, fast asleep and snoring throughout.

The legal engine, once set in motion, takes Silindu to 'the great judge', but not before he has received the consolations of religion, ministered by a wandering beggar. This noble philosopher, who knows the jungle and at whose feet Silindu prostrates himself, gives him the magic formula – a stanza in a language unintelligible to him and whose words he has difficulty in memorizing. What matter, if it stills the sighs of the oppressed and gives heart to a heartless world.

Thus fortified Silindu appears before the Supreme Court at Tangalle. What was called for on this occasion was a judge full of wisdom, understanding and compassion, as in the story of a previous birth of the Buddha which Hinnihami had remembered. What is provided is the painstakingly honest inadequacy of British justice: the blindfold figure with the avenging sword and the scales. As the writer sees it, the proceedings, despite all efforts to the contrary, become a charade: 'the pomp and greater solemnity of this court', the judge in scarlet, bewigged without doubt, the black cloth placed on his head at the dramatic moment and the accused unable to understand the mummery. The final irony comes later with the appearance of 'the Sinhalese gentleman dressed very beautifully in European clothes and a light grey helmet'. He reads aloud in a high pompous voice a document which commutes the death sentence into one of twenty years rigorous imprisonment.

The slow curtain is brought down in the final chapter on Babun dead in the jail and the undaunted Punchi Menika left alone in the village, as the jungle swallows up both it and her.

W. T. Stace, the philosopher, who like Leonard Woolf served in the Ceylon Civil Service, commented, not on the novel, but on Woolf's dissatisfaction with the colonial system: 'Justice, like efficiency is quite consistent with standing still, making no advance, having no goal, no policy, no imagination and no vision. For justice, unless the word is used in some very wide sense as practically equivalent to all virtue – means only administering the existing laws and institutions with strict impartiality and without respect of persons.'

The novel gives the clear impression that Leonard Woolf would not have been content with this. But it does not indicate where he would have liked justice to proceed or how. It is, however, as relevant today as when it first appeared in 1913. It should be better known, for, though villages like Beddagama may no longer exist, its author shows a classic level of understanding of the human situation to be met with in shanty towns, ghettoes, labour and refugee camps, and other places where the rejects of society are concentrated.

THE VILLAGE IN THE JUNGLE

CHAPTER I

THE village was called Beddagama, which means the village in the jungle. It lay in the low country or plains, midway between the sea and the great mountains which seem, far away to the north, to rise like a long wall straight up from the sea of trees. It was in, and of, the jungle; the air and smell of the jungle lay heavy upon it – the smell of hot air, of dust, and of dry and powdered leaves and sticks. Its beginning and its end was in the jungle, which stretched away from it on all sides unbroken, north and south and east and west, to the blue line of the hills and to the sea. The jungle surrounded it, overhung it, continually pressed in upon it. It stood at the door of the houses, always ready to press in upon the compounds and open spaces, to break through the mud huts, and to choke up the tracks and paths. It was only by yearly clearing with axe and katty that it could be kept out. It was a living wall about the village, a wall which, if the axe were spared, would creep in and smother and blot out the village itself.

There are people who will tell you that they have no fear of the jungle, that they know it as well as the streets of Maha Nuwara or their own compounds. Such people are either liars and boasters, or they are fools, without understanding or feeling for things as they really are. I knew such a man once, a hunter and tracker of game, a little man with hunched-up shoulders and peering, cunning little eyes, and a small dark face all pinched and lined, for he spent his life crouching, slinking, and peering through the undergrowth and the trees. He was more silent than the leopard and more cunning than the jackal: he knew the tracks better than the doe who leads the herd. He would boast that he could see a buck down wind before it could scent him, and a leopard through the thick undergrowth before it could see him. 'Why should I fear the jungle?' he would say. 'I know it better than my own compound. A few trees and bushes and

leaves, and some foolish beasts. There is nothing to fear there.'
One day he took his axe in his hand, and the sandals of deer-hide
to wear in thorny places, and he went out to search for the shed
horns of deer, which he used to sell to traders from the towns.
He never returned to the village again, and months afterwards in
thick jungle I found his bones scattered upon the ground,
beneath some thorn-bushes, gnawed by the wild pig and the
jackal, and crushed and broken by the trampling of elephants.
And among his bones lay a bunch of peacock feathers that he
had collected and tied together with a piece of creeper, and his
betel-case, and the key of his house, and the tattered fragments
of his red cloth. In the fork of one of the thorn-bushes hung his
axe: the massive wooden handle had been snapped in two. I do
not know how he died; but I know that he had boasted that
there was no fear in the jungle, and in the end the jungle took
him.

All jungles are evil, but no jungle is more evil than that which
lay about the village of Beddagama. If you climb one of the bare
rocks that jut up out of it, you will see the jungle stretched out
below you for mile upon mile on all sides. It looks like a great
sea, over which the pitiless hot wind perpetually sends waves
unbroken, except where the bare rocks, rising above it, show like
dark smudges against the grey-green of the leaves. For ten
months of the year the sun beats down and scorches it; and the
hot wind in a whirl of dust tears over it, tossing the branches and
scattering the leaves. The trees are stunted and twisted by the
drought, by the thin and sandy soil, by the dry wind. They are
scabrous, thorny trees, with grey leaves whitened by the clouds
of dust which the wind perpetually sweeps over them: their
trunks are grey with hanging, stringy lichen. And there are
enormous cactuses, evil-looking and obscene, with their great
fleshy green slabs, which put out immense needle-like spines.
More evil-looking still are the great leafless trees, which look like
a tangle of gigantic spiders' legs – smooth, bright green, jointed
together – from which, when they are broken, oozes out a milky,
viscous fluid.

And between the trees are the bushes which often knit the

whole jungle together into an impenetrable tangle of thorns. On the ground beneath the trees it is very still and very hot; for the sterile earth is covered with this thorny matted undergrowth, through which the wind cannot force its way. The sound of the great wind rushing over the tree-tops makes the silence below seem more heavy. The air is heavy with the heat beating up from the earth, and with the smell of dead leaves. All the bushes and trees seem to be perpetually dying for ten months of the year, the leaves withering, and the twigs and branches decaying and dropping off, to be powdered over the ground among the coarse withered grass and the dead and blackened shrubs. And yet every year, when the rains come, the whole jungle bursts out again into green; and it forces its way forward into any open space, upon the tracks, into villages and compounds, striving to blot out everything in its path.

If you walk all day through the jungle along its tangled tracks, you will probably see no living thing. It is so silent and still there that you might well believe that nothing lives in it. You might perhaps in the early morning hear the trumpeting and squealing of a herd of elephants, or the frightened bark of the spotted deer, or the deeper bark of the sambur, or the blaring call of the peacock. But as the day wore on, and the heat settled down upon the trees, you would hear no sound but the rush of the wind overhead, and the grating of dry branches against one another. Yet the shadows are full of living things, moving very silently, themselves like shadows, between the trees, slinking under the bushes and peering through the leaves.

For the rule of the jungle is first fear, and then hunger and thirst. There is fear everywhere: in the silence and in the shrill calls and the wild cries, in the stir of the leaves and the grating of branches, in the gloom, in the startled, slinking, peering beasts. And behind the fear is always the hunger and the thirst, and behind the hunger and the thirst fear again. The herd of deer must come down to drink at the water-hole. They come down driven by their thirst, very silently through the deep shadows of the trees to the water lying white under the moon. They glide like shadows out of the shadows, into the moonlight, hesitating, tiptoeing, throwing up their heads to stare again into the darkness, leaping back only to be goaded on again by their thirst, ears twitching to catch a sound, and nostrils quivering to catch a scent of danger. And when the black muzzles go down into the water, it is only for a moment; and then with a rush the herd scatters back again terror-stricken into the darkness. And behind the herd comes the leopard, slinking through the under-growth. Whom has he to fear? Yet there is fear in his eyes and in his slinking feet, fear in his pricked ears and in the bound with which he vanishes into the shadows at the least suspicious sound.

In the time of the rains the jungle might seem to be a pleasant place. The trees are green, and the grass stands high in the open spaces. Water lies in pools everywhere; there is no need to go stealthily by night to drink at rivers or water-holes. The deer and the pig roam away, growing fat on the grass and the young leaves and the roots; the elephant travels far from the river bank. The time of plenty lasts, however, but a little while. The wind from the north-east drops, the rain fails; for a month a great stillness lies over the jungle; the sun looks down from a cloudless sky; the burning air is untempered by a breath of wind. It is spring in the jungle, a short and fiery spring, when in a day the trees burst out into great masses of yellow or white flowers, which in a day wither and die away.

The pools and small water-holes begin to dry up under the great heat; the earth becomes caked and hard. Then the wind begins to blow from the south-west, fitfully at first, but growing steadier and stronger every day. A little rain falls, the last before the long drought sets in. The hot, dry wind sweeps over the trees. The grass and the shrubs die down; the leaves on the small trees shrivel up, and grow black and fall. The grey earth crumbles into dust, and splits beneath the sun. The little streams run dry; the great rivers shrink, until only a thin stream of water trickles slowing along in the middle of their immense beds of yellow sand. The water-holes are dry; only here and there in the very deepest of them, on the rocks, a little muddy water still remains.

Then the real nature of the jungle shows itself. Over great

tracts there is no water for the animals to drink. Only the elephants remember the great rivers, which lie far away, and whose banks they left when the rains came; as soon as the south-west wind begins to blow, they make for the rivers again. But the deer and the pig have forgotten the rivers. In the water-holes the water has sunk too low for them to reach it on the slippery rocks; for days and nights they wander round and round the holes, stretching down their heads to the water, which they cannot touch. Many die of thirst and weakness around the water-holes. From time to time one, in his efforts to reach the water, slips, and falls into the muddy pool, and in the evening the leopard finds him an easy prey. The great herds of deer roam away, tortured by thirst, through the parched jungle. They smell the scent of water in the great wind that blows in from the sea. Day after day they wander away from the rivers into the wind, south towards the sea, stopping from time to time to raise their heads and snuff in the scent of water, which draws them on. Again many die of thirst and weakness on the way; and the jackals follow the herds, and pull down in the open the fawns that their mothers are too weak to protect. And the herds wander on until at last they stand upon the barren, waterless shore of the sea.

Such is the jungle which lay about the village of Beddagama. The village consisted of ten scattered houses, mean huts made of mud plastered upon rough jungle sticks. Only one of the huts had a roof of tiles, that of the village headman Babehami; the others were covered with a thatch of cadjans, the dried leaves of the coconut-palm. Below the huts to the east of the village lay the tank, a large shallow depression in the jungle. Where the depression was deepest the villagers had raised a long narrow bund or mound of earth, so that when the rain fell the tank served as a large pond in which to store the water. Below the bund lay the stretch of rice-fields, about thirty acres, which the villagers cultivated if the tank filled with water, by cutting a hole in the bund, through which the water from the tank ran into the fields. The jungle rose high and dense around the fields and the tank; it stretched away unbroken, covering all the country except the fields, the tank, and the little piece of ground upon which the houses and compounds stood.

The villagers all belonged to the goiya caste, which is the caste of cultivators. If you had asked them what their occupation was, they would have replied 'the cultivation of rice'; but in reality they only cultivated rice about once in ten years. Rice requires water in plenty; it must stand in water for weeks before it grows ripe for the reaping. It could only be cultivated if the village tank filled with water, and much rain had to fall before the tank filled. If the rains from the north-east in November were good, and the people could borrow seed, then the rice-fields in January and February were green, and the year brought the village health and strength; for rice gives strength as does no other food. But this happened very rarely. Usually the village lived entirely by cultivating chenas. In August every man took a katty and went out into the jungle and cut down the undergrowth, over an acre or two. Then he returned home. In September he went out again and set fire to the dead undergrowth, and at night the jungle would be lit up by points of fire scattered around the village for miles; for so sterile is the earth, that a chena, burnt and sown for one year, will yield no crop again for ten years. Thus the villagers must each year find fresh jungle to burn. In October the land is cleared of ash and rubbish, and when the rains fall in November the ground is sown broadcast with millet or kurakkan or maize, with pumpkins, chillies, and a few vegetables. In February the grain is reaped, and on it the village must live until the next February. No man will ever do any other work, nor will he leave the village in search of work. But even in a good year the grain from the chenas was scarcely sufficient for the villagers. And just as in the jungle fear and hunger for ever crouch, slink, and peer with every beast, so hunger and the fear of hunger always lay upon the village. It was only for a few months each year after the crop was reaped that the villagers knew the daily comfort of a full belly. And the grain sown in chenas is an evil food, heating the blood, and bringing fever and the foulest of all diseases, parangi. There were few in the village without the filthy sores of parangi, their legs eaten out to the bone with the yellow,

sweating ulcers, upon which the flies settle in swarms. The naked
children, soon after their birth, crawled about with immense
pale yellow bellies, swollen with fever, their faces puffed with
dropsy, their arms and legs thin, twisted little sticks.

The spirit of the jungle is in the village, and in the people who
live in it. They are simple, sullen, silent men. In their faces you
can see plainly the fear and hardship of their lives. They are very
near to the animals which live in the jungle around them. They
look at you with the melancholy and patient stupidity of the
buffalo in their eyes, or the cunning of the jackal. And there is in
them the blind anger of the jungle, the ferocity of the leopard,
and the sudden fury of the bear.

In Beddagama there lived a man called Silindu, with his wife
Dingihami. They formed one of the ten families which made up
the village, and all the families were connected more or less
closely by marriage. Silindu was a cousin of the wife of
Babehami, the headman, who lived in the adjoining compound.
Babehami had been made a headman because he was the only
man in the village who could write his name. He was a very
small man, and was known as Punchi Arachchi[1] (the little
Arachchi). Years ago, when a young man, he had gone on a
pilgrimage to the vihare[2] at Medamahanuwara. He had fallen ill
there, and had stayed for a month or two in the priest's pansala.
The priest had taught him his letters, and he had learnt enough
to be able to write his own name.

Silindu was a cultivator like the other villagers. The village
called him 'tikak pissu' (slightly mad). Even in working in the
chena he was the laziest man in the village. His real occupation
was hunting; that is to say he shot deer and pig, with a long
muzzle-loading gas-pipe gun, whenever he could creep up to one
in the thick jungle; or, lying by the side of a water-hole at night,
shoot down some beast who had come there to drink. Why this
silent little man, with the pinched-up face of a grey monkey and
the long, silent, sliding step, should be thought slightly mad, was
not immediately apparent. He seemed only at first sight a little

[1] The lowest rank of headman, the headman over a village.
[2] A Buddhist temple containing an image of Buddha.

more taciturn and inert than the other villagers. But the village had its reasons. Silindu slept with his eyes open like some animals, and very often he would moan, whine, and twitch in his sleep like a dog; he slept as lightly as a deer, and would start up from the heaviest sleep in an instant fully awake. When not in the jungle he squatted all day long in the shadow of his hut, staring before him, and no one could tell whether he was asleep or awake. Often you would have to shout at him and touch him before he would attend to what you had to say. But the strangest thing about him was this, that although he knew the jungle better than any man in the whole district, and although he was always wandering through it, his fear of it was great. He never attempted to explain or to deny this fear. When other hunters laughed at him about it, all he would say was, 'I am not afraid of any animal in the jungle, no, not even of the bear or of the solitary elephant (whom all of you really fear), but I am afraid of the jungle.' But though he feared it, he loved it in a strange, unconscious way, in the same unconscious way in which the wild buffalo loves the wallow, and the leopard his lair among the rocks. Silent, inert, and sullen he worked in the chena or squatted about his compound, but when he started for the jungle he became a different man. With slightly bent knees and toes turned out, he glided through the impenetrable scrub with a long, slinking stride, which seemed to show at once both the fear and the joy in his heart.

And Silindu's passions, his anger, and his desire were strange and violent even for the jungle. It was not easy to rouse his anger; he was a quiet man, who did not easily recognise the hand which wronged him. But if he were roused he would sit for hours or days motionless in his compound, his mind moving vaguely with hatred; and then suddenly he would rise and search out his enemy, and fall upon him like a wild beast. And sometimes at night a long-drawn howl would come from Silindu's hut, and the villagers would laugh and say, 'Hark! the leopard is with his mate,' and the women next morning when they saw Dingihami drawing water from the tank would jeer at her.

At length Dingihami bore twins, two girls, of whom one was

called Punchi Menika and the other Hinnihami. When the
women told Silindu that his wife was delivered of two girls, he
rushed into the hut and began to beat his wife on the head and
breasts as she lay on the mat, crying, 'Vesi! vesi mau! Where is
the son who is to carry my gun into the jungle, and who will
clear the chena for me? Do you bear me vesi for me to feed and
clothe and provide dowries? Curse you!' And this was the
beginning of Silindu's quarrel with Babehami, the headman; for
Babehami, hearing the cries of Dingihami and the other women,
rushed up from the adjoining compound and dragged Silindu
from the house.

Dingihami died two days after giving birth to the twins.
Silindu had a sister called Karlinahami, who lived in a house at
the other end of the village. Misfortune had fallen upon her, the
misfortune so common in the life of a jungle village. Her
husband had died of fever two months before: a month later she
bore a child which lived but two weeks. When Dingihami died,
Silindu brought her to his hut to bring up his two children. Her
hut was abandoned to the jungle. When the next rains fell the
mud walls crumbled away, the tattered roof fell in, the jungle
crept forward into the compound and over the ruined walls; and
when Punchi Menika was two years old, only a little mound in
the jungle marked the place where Karlinahami's house had
stood.

Karlinahami was a short, dark, stumpy woman, with large
impassive eyes set far apart from one another, flat broad cheeks,
big breasts, and thick legs. Unlike her brother she was always
busy, sweeping the house and compound, fetching water from
the tank, cooking, and attending to the children. Very soon after
she came to Silindu's house she began to talk and think of the
children as though she had borne them herself. Like her brother
she was slow and sparing of speech; and her eyes often had in
them the look, so often in his, as if she were watching something
far away in the distance. She very rarely took much part in the
interminable gossip of the other village women when they met at
the tank or outside their huts. This gossip is always connected
with their husbands and children, food and quarrels.

But Karlinahami was noted for her story-telling: she was never very willing to begin, but often, after the evening meal had been eaten, the women and many of the men would gather in Silindu's compound to listen to one of her stories. They sat round the one room or outside round the door, very still and silent, listening to her droning voice as she squatted by the fire and stared out into the darkness. Outside lay Silindu, apparently paying no attention to the tale. The stories were either old tales which she had learnt from her mother, or were stories usually about Buddha, which she had heard told by pilgrims round the camp-fire on their way to pilgrimages, or in the madamas or pilgrims' resting-places at festivals. These tales, and a curious droning chant with which she used to sing them to sleep, were the first things that the two children remembered. This chant was peculiar to Karlinahami, and no other woman of the village used it. She had learnt it from her mother. The words ran thus:

'Sleep, child, sleep against my side,
Aiyo! aiyo! the weary way you've cried;
Hush, child, hush, pressed close against my side.

'Aiyo! aiyo! will the trees never end?
Our women's feet are weary; O Great One, send
Night on us, that our wanderings may end.

'Hush, child, hush, thy father leads the way,
Thy mother's feet are weary, but the day
Will end somewhere for the followers in the way.

'Aiyo! aiyo! the way is rough and steep,
Aiyo! the thorns and sharp, the rivers deep,
But the night comes at last. So sleep, child, sleep.'

Until Punchi Menika and Hinnihami were three years old Silindu appeared not even to be aware of their existence. He took no notice of them in the house or compound, and never spoke about them. But one day he was sitting in front of his hut staring into the jungle, when Punchi Menika crawled up to him and put her hand on his knee, and looked solemnly up into his face. Silindu looked down at her, took her by her hands, and stood her up between his two knees. He stared vacantly into her eyes for some time, and then suddenly he began to speak to her in a low voice:

'Little toad! why have you left the pond? Isn't there food there for your little belly? Rice and cocoanuts and mangoes and little cakes of kurakkan? Is the belly full, that you have left the pond for the jungle? Foolish little toad! The water is good, but the trees are evil. You have come to a bad place of dangers and devils. Yesterday, little toad, I lay under a domba-tree by the side of a track, my gun in my hand, waiting for what might pass. The devils are very angry in the jungle, for there has been no rain now for these three months. The water-holes are dry; the leaves and grass are brown; the deer are very thin; and the fawns, dropped this year, are dying of weakness and hunger and thirst. Therefore, the devils are hungry, and there is nothing more terrible than a hungry devil. Well, there I lay, flat on the ground, with my gun in my hand; and I saw on the opposite side of the track, lying under a domba-tree, a leopardess waiting for what might pass. I put down my gun, and, "Sister," I said, "is the belly empty?" For her coat was mangy, and the belly caught up below, as though with pain. "Yakko, he-devil," she answered, "three days now I have killed but one thin grey monkey, and there are two cubs in the cave to be fed." "Yakkini, she-devil," I said, "there are two little toads at home to be fed. But I still have a handful of kurakkan in my hut, from which my sister can make cakes. It remains from last year's chena, and after it is eaten there will be nothing. The headman, too, is pressing for the three shillings[1] body tax. 'How,' I say to him, 'can there be money where there is not even food?' But the kurakkan will last until next poya day. Therefore, your hunger is greater than mine. The first kill is yours." So we lay still a long time, and at last I heard far away the sound of a hoof upon a dry stick. "Sister," I whispered, "I hear a deer coming this way." "Yakko, have you no ears?" she said. "A long while now I have been listening to a

---

[1] Shilling used colloquially for the half rupee or 50 cents = 5p.

herd of wild pig coming down wind. Can you not even now hear their strong breathing, and their rooting in the dry earth, and the patter of the young ones' feet on the dry leaves?" "Yakkini," I said, for I heard her teeth clicking in the darkness, "the ear of the hungry is in the belly: the sound of your teeth can be heard a hoo[1] cry's distance away." So we lay still again, and at last the herd of pigs came down the track. First came an old boar, very black, his tusks shining white in the shadows; then many sows and young boars; and here and there the little pigs running in and out among the sows. And as they passed, one of the little pigs ran out near the domba-bush, and Yakkini sprang and caught it in her teeth, and leapt with it into the branch of a palu-tree which overhung the path. There she sat, and the little pig in her mouth screamed to its mother. Then all the little pigs ran together screaming, and stood on one side, near the bush where I lay; and the great boars and the young boars and sows ran round the palu-tree, looking up at Yakkini, and making a great noise. And the old sow, who had borne the little pig in Yakkini's mouth, put her forefeet against the trunk of the tree, and looked up, and said, "Come down, Yakkini; she-devil, thief. Are you afraid of an old, tuskless sow? Come down." But the leopardess laughed, and bit the little pig in the back behind the head until it died, and she called down to the old sow, "Go your way, mother. There are two cubs at home in the cave, and they are very hungry. Every year I drop but one or two cubs in the cave, but the whole jungle swarms with your spawn. I see eight brothers and sisters of your child there by the domba-bush. Go your way, lest I choose another for my mate. Also, I do not like your man's teeth." The old boar and the sows were very angry, and for a long while they ran round the tree, and tore at it with their tusks, and looked up and cursed Yakkini. But Yakkini sat and watched them, and licked the blood which dripped from the little pig's back. I too lay very still under my domba-bush, for there is danger in an angry herd. At last the old boar became tired, and he gathered the little pigs together in the middle of the

---

[1] A common method of measuring distance – the distance being that at which it is possible to hear a man cry 'hoo'.

herd, and led them away down the track. Then Yakkini dropped to the ground, and bounded away into the jungle, carrying the little pig in her mouth. So you see, little crow, it is a bad place to which you have come. Be careful, or some other devil will drop on you out of a bush, and carry you off in his mouth.'

While Silindu had been speaking, Hinnihami had crawled and tottered across the compound to join her sister. At the end of his long story she was leaning against his shoulder. From that day he seemed to regard the two children differently from the rest of the world in which he lived. He was never tired of pouring out to them in a low, monotonous drone his thoughts, opinions, and doings. That they did not understand a word of what he said did not trouble him in the least; but when they grew old enough to understand and to speak and to question him, he began to take a new pleasure in explaining to them the world in which he lived.

It was a strange world, a world of bare and brutal facts, of superstition, of grotesque imagination; a world of trees and the perpetual twilight of their shade; a world of hunger and fear and devils, where a man was helpless before the unseen and unintelligible powers surrounding him. He would go over to them again and again in the season of drought the reckoning of his small store of grain, and the near approach of the time when it would be exhausted; his perpetual fear of hunger; his means and plans for obtaining just enough for existence until the next chena season. But, above all, his pleasure seemed to be to tell them of the jungle, of his wanderings in search of game, of his watchings by the water-holes at night, of the animals and devils which lived among its shadows.

CHAPTER II

So Punchi Menika and Hinnihami grew up to be somewhat different from the other village children, who crawl and play about the compounds, always with the women and always listening to women's gossip. Long before they had grown strong and big enough to go down in the morning and evening with Karlinahami to the tank, and to carry back on their heads the red earthenware waterpots, they had learnt from Silindu to sit by his side for hour upon hour through the hot afternoons, very still and very silent, while he stared silently before him, or droned out his interminable tales. They grew up to be strange and silent children, sitting one on either side of him in a long, thoughtless trance. And they learnt to believe all he told them about the strange world of jungle which surrounded them, the world of devils, animals, and trees. But above all they learnt to love him, blindly, as a dog loves his master.

When they grew old enough to trot along by his side, Silindu used to take them out with him into the jungle. The villagers were astonished and shocked, but Silindu went his own way. He showed them the water-holes upon the rocks; the thick jungle where the elephant hides himself from the heat of the day, strolling leisurely among the trees and breaking off great branches to feed upon the leaves as he strolls; the wallow of the buffalo, and the caves where the bear and the leopard make their lairs. He showed them the sambur lying during the day in the other great caves; they dashed out, tens and tens of them, like enormous bats from the shadow of the over-hanging rocks, to disappear with a crash into the jungle below. He taught them to walk so that no leaf rustled or twig snapped under their feet, to creep up close to the deer and the sambur and the pig. They were surprised at first that the animals in the jungle did not speak to them as they always did to Silindu when he was alone. But Silindu explained it to them. 'You are very young,' he said. 'You do not know the tracks. You are strange to the beasts. But they know me. I have grown old among the tracks. A man must live many years in the jungle before the beasts speak to him, or he can understand what they say.'

Punchi Menika and Hinnihami were also unlike the other village children in appearance. They, like Silindu, never had fever, and even in the days of greatest scarcity Karlinahami had seen that they got food. Karlinahami was far more careful to wash them than most mothers are: she used to quote the saying, 'Dirt is bad and children are trouble, but a dirty child is the worst of troubles.' The result was that they never got parangi, or the swollen belly and pale skin of fever. Their skin was smooth and blooming; it shone with a golden colour, like the coat of a fawn when the sun shines on it. Their eyes were large and melancholy; like the eyes of Buddha in the Jataka, 'they were like two windows made of sapphire shining in a golden palace.' Their limbs were strong and straight, for their wanderings with Silindu had made their muscles firm as a man's not soft like the women's who sit about in the compound, cooking and gossiping and sleeping all day.

There was therefore considerable jealousy among the women, and ill-feeling against Karlinahami, when they saw how her foster children were growing up. When they were ten or eleven years old, it often burst out against her in angry taunts at the tank.

'O Karlinahami!' Nanchohami, the headman's wife, would say, 'you are growing an old woman and, alas, childless! But you have done much for your brother's children. Shameless they must be to leave it to you to fetch the water from the tank and not to help you. This is the fourth chatty full you are carrying to-day. I have seen it with these eyes. The lot of the childless woman is a hard one. See how my little one of eight years helps me!'

'Nanchohami, your tongue is still as sharp as chillies. Punchi Menika has gone with my brother, and Hinnihami is busy in the house.'

'Punchi Menika want but three things to make her a man. I

pity you, Karlinahami, to live in the house of a madman, and to
bring up his children shameless, having no children of your own.
They are vedda[1] children, and will be vedda women, wandering
in the jungle like men.'

The other women laughed, and Angohami, a dirty shrivelled
woman, with thin shrivelled breasts, called out in a shrill voice:

'Why should we suffer these veddas in the village? Their
compound smells of their own droppings, and of the offal and
rotten meat on which they feed. I have borne six children, and
the last died but yesterday. In the morning he was well: then
Silindu cast the evil eye upon him as he passed our door, and in
the evening he was dead. They wither our children that their
own may thrive.'

'You lie,' said Karlinahami, roused for the moment by this
abuse; 'you lie, mother of dirt. Yesterday at this hour I saw your
Podi Sinho here in the tank, pale and shivering with fever, and
pouring the cold tank water over himself. How should such a
mother keep her children? All know that you have borne six, and
that all are dead. What did you ever give them but foul words?'

'Go and lie with your brother, the madman, the vedda, the
pariah,' shrieked Angohami as Karlinahami turned to go. 'Go to
your brother of the evil eye. You blighter of others' children,
eater of offal, vesi, vesige mau! Go to him of the evil eye, belli,
bellige duwa; go to your brother. Aiyo! aiyo! My little Podi
Sinho! I am a mother only of the dead, a mother of six dead
children. Look at my breasts, shrivelled and milkless. I say to the
father of my child,[2] "Father of Podi Sinho," I say, "there is no
kurakkan in the house, there is no millet and no pumpkin, not
even a pinch of salt. Three days now I have eaten nothing but
jungle leaves. There is no milk in my breasts for the child." Then
I get foul words and blows. "Does the rain come in August?" he
says. "Can I make the kurakkan flower in July? Hold your

---

[1] The veddas are the aborigines of Ceylon, and are or were hunters. They are
often identified with Yakkas or devils.

[2] A Sinhalese woman will not speak to or refer to her husband by name. She
always speaks of or to him as 'The father of my child,' or 'The father of Podi
Sinho, etc., or simply 'He.'

tongue, you fool. August is the month in which the children die. What can I do?" Then comes fever and Silindu's evil eye, curse him, and the little ones die. Aiyo! aiyo!'

'Your man is right,' said Nanchohami. 'This is the month when the children die. Last year in this month I buried one and my brother's wife another. Good rain never falls now, and there is always hunger and fever. The old die and the little ones with them. The father of my children has but nine houses under him, and makes but five shillings a year from his headmanship. His father's father, who was headman before him, had thirty houses in his headmanship, and twenty shillings were paid him by the Government every year, besides twenty-four kurunies[1] of paddy from the fields below the tank. I have not seen rice these five years. The headman now gives all and receives nothing.' Here one of the women laughed. 'You may well laugh, Podi Nona,' she continued. 'Did not he[2] lend your man last year twenty kurunies of kurakkan,[3] and has a grain of it come back to our house? And Silindu owes another thirty, and came but yesterday for more. And Angohami there, who whines about her Podi Sinho, her man has had twenty-five kurunies since the reaping of the last crop.'

These words of Nanchohami were not without effect. An uneasy movement began among the little group of women at the mention of debts; clothes were gathered up, the chatties of water placed on their heads, and they began to move away out of reach of the sharp tongue of the headman's wife. And as they moved away up the small path, which led from the tank to the compounds, they murmured together that Nanchohami did not seem to remember that they had to repay two kurunies of kurakkan for every kuruni lent to them.

Nanchohami had touched the mainspring upon which the life of the village worked – debt. The villagers lived upon debt, and their debts were the main topic of their conversation. A good kurakkan crop, from two to four acres of chena, would be

---

[1] Kuruni is a measure employed in the measurement of grain.
[2] *Vide* note 2 on p.18.
[3] Kurakkan, a grain, *Eleusine coracana*.

sufficient to support a family for a year. But no one, not even the headman, ever enjoyed the full crop which he had reaped. At the time of reaping a band of strangers from the little town of Kamburupitiya, thirty miles away, would come into the village. Mohamadu Lebbe Ahamadu Cassim, the Moorman boutique-keeper, had supplied clothes to be paid for in grain, with a hundred per cent. interest, at the time of reaping; the fat Sinhalese Mudalali,[1] Kodikarage Allis Appu, had supplied grain and curry stuffs on the same terms; and among a crowd of smaller men the sly-faced low-caste man, who called himself Achchige Don Andris (his real name Andrissa would have revealed his caste), who, dressed in dirty white European trousers and a coat, was the agent of the tavern-keeper in Kamburupitiya, from whom the villagers had taken on credit the native spirit, made from the juice of the cocoanut flowers, to be drunk at the time of marriages. The villagers neither obtained nor expected any pity from this horde. With the reaping of the chenas came the settlement of debts. With their little greasy notebooks, full of unintelligible letters and figures, they descended upon the chenas; and after calculations, wranglings, and abuse, which lasted for hour after hour, the accounts were settled, and the strangers left the village, their carts loaded with pumpkins, sacks of grain, and not unfrequently the stalks of Indian hemp,[2] which by Government order no man may grow or possess, for the man that smokes it becomes mad. And when the strangers had gone, the settlement with the headman began; for the headman, on a small scale, lent grain on the same terms in times of scarcity, or when seed was wanted to sow the chenas.

In the end the villager carried but little grain from his chena to his hut. Very soon after the reaping of the crop he was again at the headman's door, begging for a little kurakkan to be repaid at the next harvest, or tramping the thirty miles to Kamburupitiya to hang about the bazaar, until the Mudalali agreed once more, to enter his name in the greasy notebook.

With the traders in Kamburupitiya the transactions were

---

[1] Term applied usually to a rich trader.
[2] Called bhang, ganja, or hashish.

purely matters of business, but with the headman the whole village recognised that they were something more. It was a very good thing for Babehami, the Arachchi, to feel that Silindu owed him many kurunies of kurakkan which he could not repay. When Babehami wanted some one to clear a chena for him, he asked Silindu to do it; and Silindu, remembering the debt, dared not refuse. When Silindu shot a deer — for which offence the Arachchi should have brought him before the police court at Kamburupitiya — he remembered his debt, and the first thing he did was to carry the best piece of meat as an offering to the headman's house. And Babehami was a quiet, cunning man in the village: he never threatened, and rarely talked of his loans to his debtors, but there were few in the village who dared to cross him, and who did not feel hanging over them the power of the little man.

The power which they felt hanging over them was by no means imaginary; it could make the life of the man who offended the headman extremely unpleasant. It was not only by his loans that Babehami had his hand upon the villagers; their daily life could be made smooth or difficult by him at every turn.

The life of the village and of every man in it depended upon the cultivation of chenas. A chena is merely a piece of jungle, which every ten years is cleared of trees and undergrowth and sown with grain broadcast and with vegetables. The villagers owned no jungle themselves; it belonged to the Crown, and no one might fell a tree or clear a chena in it without a permit from the Government. It was through these permits that the headman had his hold upon the villagers. Application for one had to be made through him; it was he who reported if a clearing had been made without one, or if a man, having been given one, cleared more jungle than it allowed him to clear. Every one in the village knew well that Babehami's friends would find no difficulty in obtaining the authority to clear a chena, and that the Agent Hamadoru[1] would never hear from Babehami whether they had

---

[1] The head of a district for administrative and revenue purposes is a European Civil servant, and is called an assistant Government agent. The Sinhalese call him Agent Hamadoru.

cleared four acres or eight. But the life of the unfortunate man, who had offended the headman, would be full of dangers and difficulties. The permit applied for by him would be very slow in reaching his hands: when it did reach his hands, if he cleared half an acre more than it allowed him to clear, his fine would be heavy; and woe betide him if he rashly cleared a chena without a permit at all.

Babehami had never liked Silindu, who was a bad debtor. Silindu was too lazy even to cultivate a chena properly, and even in a good year his crop was always the smallest in the village. He was always in want, and always borrowing; and Babehami found it no easy task to gather in principal and interest after the boutique-keepers from Kamburupitiya had taken their dues. And he was not an easy man to argue with: if he wanted a loan he would, unheeding of any excuse or refusal, hang about the headman's door for a whole day. But if it were a case of repayment, he would sit staring over his creditor's head, listening, without a sign or a word, to the quiet persuasive arguments of the headman.

The headman's dislike became more distinct after the birth of Punchi Menika and Hinnihami. Silindu had resented his interference between him and his wife, and when Dingihami died bitter words had passed between them. Though Silindu soon forgot them, Babehami did not. For years Silindu did not realise what was taking place, but he vaguely felt that life was becoming harder for him. A month after Dingihami's death his store of grain was exhausted, and it became necessary for him to begin his yearly borrowings. Accordingly, he took his gun and went in the evening to the nearest water-hole to wait for deer. The first night he was unsuccessful: no deer came to drink; but on the second he shot a doe. He skinned the deer, cut it up, and carried the meat to his hut. He then carefully chose the best piece of meat, and took it with him to Babehami's house. The headman was squatting in his doorway chewing betel. His little eyes twinkled when he saw Silindu with the meat.

'Ralahami,'[1] said Silindu, stopping just outside the door,

[1] A respectful form of address.

'yesterday I was in the jungle collecting domba fruit – what else is there to eat? – when I smelt a smell of something dead some fathoms away. I searched about, and soon I came upon the carcase of a doe killed by a leopard – the marks of his claws were under the neck, and the belly was eaten. The meat I have brought to my house. This piece is for you.'

The headman took the meat in silence, and hung it up in the house. He fetched a chew of betel and gave it to Silindu. The two men then squatted down, one on each side of the door. For a long time neither spoke: their chewing was only interrupted every now and then by the ejection of a jet of red saliva. At last Babehami broke the silence:

'Four days ago I was in Kamburupitiya – I was called to the kachcheri there. They asked me two fanams[1] in the bazaar for a cocoanut.'

'Aiyo! I have not seen a cocoanut for two years.'

'Two fanams! And last year at this time they were but one fanam each. In the bazaar I met the Korala Mahatmaya. The Korala Mahatmaya is a hard man: he said to me, "Arachchi, there are guns in your village for which no permit has been given by the Agent Hamadoru." I said to him, "Ralahami, if there be, the fault is not mine." Then he said, "The order has come from the Agent Hamadoru to the Dissa Mahatmaya[2] that if one gun be found without permit in a headman's village there will be trouble both for the Arachchi and the Korala." Now the Dissa Mahatmaya is a good man, but the Korala is hard; and they say in Kamburupitiya that the Agent Hamadoru is very hard and strict, and goes round the villages searching for guns for which no permits have been given. They say, too, that he will come this way next month.'

There was a short silence, and then Babehami continued:

'It is five months, Silindu, since I told you to take a permit for your gun, and you have not done so yet. The time to pay three

[1] A fanam: six cents, one penny.
[2] Dissa Mahatmaya is the title used by villagers in referring to chief headmen or Ratemahatmayas. Koralas are subordinate headmen of koralès under the Ratemahatmayas. Each Korala again has under him several Arachchis, who are headmen of single villages.

shillings has gone by, and you will now have to pay four. The Korala is a hard man, and the Agent Hamadoru will come next month.'

Silindu salaamed.

'Ralahami, I am a poor man. How can I pay four shillings or even three? There is not a fanam in the house. There was a permit taken two years ago. You are my father and my mother. I will hide the gun in a place that only I know of, and if it be taken or question be made, is it not easy to say that the stock was broken, and it was not considered necessary to take a permit for a broken gun?'

But the argument, which before had been successful with Babehami, now seemed to have lost its strength.

'A permit is required. It is the order of Government. I have told you the Korala is a hard man, and he is angry with me because I brought him but two cocoanuts as a present, whereas other Arachchis bring him an amunam of paddy. For I, too, am a poor man.'

Silindu sat in helpless silence. The hopelessness of raising two rupees to pay for a gun licence for the moment drove out of his mind the object of his coming to Babehami's house. All that he felt was the misery of a new misfortune, and, as was his nature, he sat dumb under it. At last, however, the pressing need of the moment again recurred to him, and he started in the tortuous way, habitual to villagers, to approach the subject.

'Ralahami, is there any objection to my clearing Nugagahahena next chena season?'

'There are three months before the chena season. Why think of that now?'

'When the belly is empty, the mouth talks of rice. Last year my chena crop was bad. There was but little rain, and the elephants broke in and destroyed much kurakkan. The Lord Buddha himself would be powerless against the elephants.'

Silindu got up as if to go. He took a step towards the stile which led into the compound, and then turned back as if he had just remembered something, and began in a soft, wheedling voice:

'Ralahami, there is nothing to eat in the house. There is Karlinahami to feed too. If you could but lend me ten kurunies! I would repay it twofold at the reaping of Nugagahahena.'

Babehami chewed for some minutes, and then spat with great deliberation.

'I have no grain to lend now, Silindu.'

'Ralahami, it is only ten kurunies I am asking for – only ten kurunies – and surely the barn behind your house is full.'

'There is very little grain in the barn now, and what there is will not last me until the reaping of the next crop. There is the old man, my father, to be fed, and my wife and her brother, and the two children.'

'Will you let me die of hunger? and my two children? Give but five kurunies, and I will repay it threefold.'

'If you had come last poya, Silindu, I could have given it. But I owed fifteen rupees to Nandiyas, the boutique-keeper in Kamburupitiya, for clothes, and I took kurakkan to pay it. The barn is all but empty.'

'Aiyo! We must die of hunger then. Give but one measure, and I will repay one kuruni at next reaping.'

'I paid away all my grain that was in the barn. The grain which remains is my father's, and he keeps it for his use. You must go to the Mudalali in Kamburupitiya, Silindu and borrow from him. And when you go there, remember, you must take a permit for the gun.'

Silindu felt that he had nothing more to say. He had the meat at home which he would dry and take to Kamburupitiya and sell in the bazaar. Then he would have to borrow from the Mudalali, who knew him too well to give anything but ruinous terms. Perhaps in that way he would manage to return to the village with a few kurunies of kurakkan and a gun licence. He walked slowly away from the headman's compound. Babehami's little eyes twinkled as he saw Silindu move away, and he smiled to himself.

CHAPTER III

SILINDU made the journey to Kamburupitiya, obtained the licence for his gun and some grain, but life continued to become harder for him. The headman's ill-feeling worked against him unostentatiously, and in all sorts of little things. He never thought about the motives and intentions of those around him, and Babehami always had some excuse for refusing a loan or pressing for payment of the body tax. He did not become conscious of Babehami's enmity, or aware that many of the difficulties of his life were due to it.

The collection of the body tax was a good example of the way in which the headman worked against him. Every villager had to pay the three-shilling tax or do work on the roads, work which was the worst of hardships to them. It had always been Babehami's custom to pay himself the tax for each villager, and then recover what he had paid, with heavy interest, out of the crops at the time of reaping. But for some years after Dingihami's death, Silindu found that when the time to pay the tax came round, Babehami was always short of money. Silindu never had any money himself, and he was therefore compelled to work upon the roads.

As the years passed he became more sullen, more taciturn, and more lazy. Some evil power – one of the unseen powers which he could not understand – was, he felt, perpetually working against him. He tried to escape from it, or at any rate to forget it by leaving the village for the jungle. He would disappear for days together into the jungle, living upon roots and the fruit of jungle trees, and anything which might fall to his gun. He talked with no one except Punchi Menika and Hinnihami. For them he never had a harsh word, and it was seldom that he returned to the hut without bringing them some wild fruit or a comb of the wild honey.

Gradually the hut of the veddas, as they were nicknamed,

seemed to the other villagers to fall under a cloud. The head-man's enmity and the strange ways of Silindu formed a bar to intercourse. And so it came about that Punchi Menika and Hinnihami grew up somewhat outside the ordinary life of the village. The strangeness and wildness of their father hung about them: as the other women said of them, they grew up in the jungle and not in the village. But with their strangeness and wildness went a simplicity of mind and of speech, which showed in many ways, but above all in their love for Silindu and each other.

Their lives were harder even than those of the other village women. As they became older the fear of hunger became more and more present with them. When Silindu was away from the village they were often compelled to live upon the fruits and leaves and roots, which they gathered themselves in the jungle. And when the chena season began, they worked like the men and boys in the chenas. They cut down the undergrowth and burnt it; they cleared the ground and sowed the grain; they lay out all night in the watch huts to scare away the deer and wild pig which came to damage the crop.

When they were fifteen, Babun Appu, the brother of Nancho-hami, came to live in his brother-in-law's, the headman's, house. He had previously lived in another house with his father, an old man, toothless and brainless. When the old man whom he had supported died, he abandoned his hut and came to live with his sister and her husband. The number of houses in the village thus sank to eight.

At that time Babun Appu was twenty-one years old. He was tall for a Sinhalese, broad-shouldered, and big-boned. His skin was a dark chocolate-brown, his face oval, his nose small, his lips full and sensual. His expression was curiously virile and simple; but his brown eyes, which were large and oval-shaped, swept it at moments with something soft, languorous, and feminine. This impression of a mixture of virility and femininity was heightened by the long hair, which he tied in a knot at the back of his head after the custom of villagers. He was noted for his strength, his energy, and his good humour. The minds of most villagers are extraordinarily tortuous and suspicious, but Babun was remarkable for his simplicity. It used to be said of him in the village, 'Babun Appu could not cheat a child; but a child, who had not learnt to talk, could cheat Babun Appu.'

For two years Babun had lived in the hut adjoining Silindu's without ever speaking more than a word or two to Punchi Menika. But her presence began to move him strongly. His lips parted, and his breathing became fast and deep as he saw her move about the compound. He watched in painful excitement her swelling breasts and the fair skin, which went into soft folds at her hips when she bent down for anything.

One night in the chena season Punchi Menika had been watching the crop of her father's chena. It lay three miles away from the village, at some distance from any other chena. The track therefore which led from it to the village was used by no one except herself, her father, and sister. In the early morning she started back to the hut.

There had been rain during the night, and the jungle was fresh and green. That freshness, which the time of rain brings for so brief a time, was upon all things. The jungle was golden with the great hanging clusters of the cassia flowers. The bushes were starred with the white karambu flowers, and splashed with masses of white and purple kettan. The grey monkeys leapt, shrieking and mocking, from bough to bough; the jungle was filled with the calling of the jungle fowl and the wild cries of the peacocks. From the distance came the trumpeting and shrieking of a herd of elephants. As Punchi Menika passed a bush she heard from behind it the clashing of horns. Very quietly she peered round. Two stags were fighting, the tines of the horns interlocked; up and down, backwards and forwards, snorting, panting, and straining they struggled for the doe which stood grazing quietly beside. Punchi Menika had crept up very quietly; but the doe became uneasy, lifted her head, and looked intently at the bush behind which Punchi Menika crouched. She approached the bush slowly, stamping the ground angrily from time to time, and uttering the sharp shrill call of alarm. But the bucks fought on, up and down the open space. Punchi Menika laughed as she turned away. 'Fear nothing, sister,' she said, 'there is no leopard crouching for you. Fight on, brothers, for the prize is fair.'

Punchi Menika walked slowly on down the track. The blood in her veins moved strangely, stirred by the stirring life around her. The trumpet call of the sambur blared through the jungle, a terrific cry of desire. The girl, who had heard it unmoved thousands of times before, started at the sound of it. A sense of uneasiness came over her. Suddenly she stopped at the sight of something which moved behind a bush down the track.

She stood trembling as Babun came out of the jungle and walked towards her. His eyes were very bright; his teeth showed white between his parted lips; the long black hair upon his breast glistened with sweat. He stood in front of her.

'Punchi Menika,' he said, 'I have come to you.'

'Aiyo!' she answered. 'I was very frightened. I thought you were a devil of the trees crouching there for me behind the bushes. Even when we were little children our father warned us against the devils that would leap upon us from the bushes.'

'I have come to you. Come with me out of the path into the thick jungle. Last night I could not sleep for thinking of you. So I came in the early morning along the path to meet you on your way from the chena. I cannot sleep, Punchi Menika, for thinking of you. I have watched you in the compound and at the tank — your fair skin and the little breasts. Do not fear, I will not hurt you, Punchi Menika; but come, come quickly, out of the path.'

A strange feeling of excitement came over the girl, of joy and fear, as Babun leant towards her, and put out his hand to take her by the wrist. A great desire to fly from him, and at the same time to be caught by him came over her. She stood looking down until his fingers touched her skin; then with a cry she broke from him, and ran down the track to the village. She heard his breathing very close to her as she ran; and when she looked round over her shoulder she felt his breath on her face, saw his bright eyes and great lips, through which the teeth shone white. Another moment and she felt the great strength of his arms as he seized her. He held her close to him by the wrists.

'Why do you run, why are you frightened, Punchi Menika? I will not hurt you.'

She allowed him to take her into the thick jungle, but she struggled with him, and her whole body shook with fear and desire as she felt his hands upon her breasts. A cry broke from her, in which joy and desire mingled with the fear and the pain:

'Aiyo! aiyo!'

CHAPTER IV

In towns and large villages there are, especially among people of the higher castes, many rigid customs and formalities regarding marriages always observed. It is true that the exclusion of women no longer exists; but young girls after puberty are supposed to be kept within the house, and only to meet men of the immediate family. A marriage is arranged formally: a formal proposal is made by the man's father or mother to the girl's father or mother. There are usually long negotiations and bargainings between the two families over the dowry. When at last the preliminaries are settled and the wedding day arrives, it is a very solemn and formal affair. All the members of each family are invited; the bridegroom goes with his friends and relations to the house of the bride, and then conducts her in procession, followed by the guests, to his own house. Much money is spent upon entertaining, and new clothes and presents.

But in villages like Beddagama, these customs and formalities are often not observed. The young girls are not kept within the house; they have to work. The young men know them, and often choose for themselves. There is no family arrangement, no formal proposal of marriage; the villagers are too poor for there to be any question of a dowry.

And yet the villager makes a clear distinction between marriage and what he calls concubinage. In the former the woman is recognised by his and her families as his wife; almost invariably she is openly taken to his house, and there is a procession and feasting on the wedding day: in the latter the woman is never publicly recognised as a wife. Marriage is considered to be more respectable than concubinage, and in a headman's immediate family it would be more usual to find the women 'recognised' wives than 'unrecognised' wives. And though in the ordinary village life the 'unrecognised' wife is as common as, or even more common than, the 'recognised' wife, and is treated by all exactly as if she were the man's wife, yet the distinction is understood and becomes apparent upon formal occasions. For instance, a woman who is living with a man as his 'unrecognised' wife cannot be present at her sister's wedding. When a man takes a woman to live with him in this informal way, the arrangement is, however, regarded as in many ways a formal one, a slightly lower form than the recognised marriage. The man and the woman are of the same caste always: there would even be strong objection on the part of the man or woman's relations if either the one or the other did not come from a 'respectable' family.

Babun knew well his brother-in-law's dislike of Silindu, and the contempt with which the 'veddas' were regarded by the other villagers. He knew that his sister and Babehami would be very angry with him if he chose a wife from such a family. But he had watched Punchi Menika, and gradually a love, which was more than mere desire, had grown up in him. The wildness and strangeness of her father and of Hinnihami were tempered in her by a wonderful gentleness. Passion and desire were strong in him: they would allow no interference with his determination to take her to live with him.

The night after his meeting with Punchi Menika on the path from the chena, he broke the news to Nanchohami and Babehami, as he and his brother-in-law were eating the evening meal.

'Sister,' he said, 'it is time that I took a wife.'

Nanchohami laughed. 'There is no difficulty. When you go to the chena the women look after you and smile and say, "Chi! chi! There goes a man. O that he would take my daughter to his house." But there are no women for you here. They are all sickly things, unfit to bear you children.'

'My father's brother married a woman of Kotegoda,' said Babehami. 'In those days wives brought dowries with them – of land. He went to live on her land at Kotegoda: it lies fifty miles away, towards Ruhuna. His sons and daughters are married now in that village, and have children. They are rich: it is a good village: rain falls there, and there are cocoanut lands, and paddy grows. The village spreads and prospers, and the headman is a rich man. They say that tax is paid upon sixty men every year. It would be a good thing for you to take a wife from there, for she would bring you a dowry.'

'Yes,' said Nanchohami, 'it would be a good thing for you to go to Kotegoda and take a woman from there, a daughter of my man's brother.[1] She would bring you land, and you could settle there. What use is it to live in this village? Even the chena crops wither for want of rain. It is an evil place this.'

'I want no woman of Kotegoda,' said Babun. 'Nor will I leave the village. There is a woman, this Punchi Menika, the daughter of Silindu. I am going to take her to live with me.'

Babehami looked at his brother-in-law, his little eyes moving restlessly in astonishment and anger. Nanchohami threw up her hands, and began in a voice which shrilled and fluted with anger:

'Ohé! So we are to take veddas into the house, and I am to call a pariah sister! A fine and a rich wife! A pariah woman, a vedda, a daughter of a dog, vesi, vesige duwa? Ohé! the headman's brother is to marry a sweeper of jakes! Do you hear this? Will you allow these Tamils[2] in your house? Yes, 'twill be a fine thing in the village to hear that the headman has given his wife and daughters to Rodiyas,[3] leopards, jackals!'

Babehami broke in upon his wife's abuse; but she, now thoroughly aroused, continued throughout the conversation to pour out a stream of foul words from the background in a voice which gradually rose shriller and shriller.

'The woman is right,' Babehami said angrily to Babun. 'You cannot bring this woman to the house.'

'I will take no other woman. I have watched her there about the compound. She is fair and gentle. She is unlike the other women of this village (here he looked round at Nanchohami), in whose mouths are always foul words.'

Babehami tried to hide his anger. He knew his brother-in-law to be obstinate as well as good-humoured and simple.

'No doubt the woman is fair. But if you desire her, is she not free to all to take? Does she not wander, like a man, in the

---

[1] The son of a paternal uncle is regarded as a brother.
[2] A favourite form of abuse among the Sinhalese is to call some one a Tamil.
[3] Rodiyas are the lowest Sinhalese caste.

jungle? They say that even kings have desired Rodiya women. If you desire her, it is not hard to take her. But there need be no talk of marriage, or bringing her to the house.'

'This morning I took her with me into the jungle, but it is not enough; the desire is still with me. I have thought about it. It is time that I took a wife to cook my food and bear me children. I want no other than this. I can leave your compound, and build myself a new house, and take her to live with me.'

Babehami's anger began to break out again.

'Are you a fool? Will you take this beggar woman to be your wife? Is not her father always about my door crying for a handful of kurakkan? Fool! I tell you my brother's children in Kotegoda will bring you land, paddy land, and cocoanuts. There is no difference between one woman and another.'

'I tell you I want no Kotegoda woman. I will take the daughter of Silindu. I want no strange woman or strange village. I can build myself a house here, and clear chenas, as my father did and his father.'

'Is it for this I took you into my house? Two years you have eaten my food. How much of my kurakkan have you taken?'

'I have taken nothing from you. I have worked two years in the chena, and the crop came to you, not to me. Is not the grain now in your barn from the chena cleared by me?'

Babehami was too quiet and cunning often to give way to anger, but this time he was carried away by the defiance of his brother-in-law, whom he regarded as a fool. He gesticulated wildly:

'Out of my house, dog; out of my house. You shall bring no woman to my compound. Go and lie with the pariahs in their own filth!'

Babun got up and stood over Babehami.

'I am going,' he said quietly, 'and I will take Punchi Menika as my wife.'

The abuse of the headman and his wife followed him out of the compound. He walked slowly over to Silindu's hut. He found Silindu squatting under a ragged mustard-tree which stood in the compound, and he squatted down by his side. He did not like Silindu; he had always an uncomfortable feeling in the presence of this wild man, who never spoke to any one unless he was spoken to; and he felt it difficult to begin now upon the subject which had brought him to the compound. Silindu paid no attention to him. Babun sat there unable to begin, listening to the sounds of the women in the hut. At last he said:

'Silindu, I have come to speak to you about your daughter Punchi Menika.'

Silindu remained quite still: he apparently had not heard. Babun touched him on the arm.

'I am talking of your daughter, Silindu, Punchi Menika.'

Silindu turned and looked at him.

'The girl is in the house. What have you to do with her?'

'I want you to listen to me, Silindu, for there is much to say. I have watched the girl from the headman's compound, and a charm has come upon me. I cannot eat or sleep for thinking of her. So I said to my sister and my sister's husband, "It is time for me to take a wife, and now I will bring this girl into the compound." But they were very angry, for they want to marry me to a woman of Kotegoda, because of the land which she would bring as dowry. To-night they abused me, and there was a quarrel. I have left their compound. Now I will make myself a house in the old compound where my father lived, and I will take the girl there as my wife.'

Silindu had become more and more attentive as he listened to Babun. The words seemed to distress him: he shifted about, fidgeted with his hands, scratched himself all over his body. When Babun stopped, he took some time before he said:

'The girl is too young to be given to a man.

Babun laughed. 'The girl has attained her age. She is older than many a woman who has a husband.'

'The girl is too young. I cannot give her to you, or evil will come of it.'

Babun's patience began to be exhausted. His good humour had been undisturbed during the scene in the headman's compound, but this new obstacle began to rouse him. His voice rose:

'I cannot live without the girl. I have quarrelled with my sister and the headman over her; I have left the compound for her. I ask no dowry. Why should you refuse her to me?'

'They call us veddas in the village, while you are of the headman's house. Does the leopard of the jungle mate with the dog of the village?'

'That is nothing to me. The wild buffalo seeks the cows in the village herds. The girl is very gentle, and my mind is made up. Also the girl wishes to come to me.'

The loud voices of the two men had reached the women in the house. They had come out, and stood listening behind the men. At the last words of Babun, Silindu cried out as if he had been struck:

'Aiyo! aiyo! they take even my daughter from me. Is there money in the house? No. Is there rice? No. Is there kurakkan, or chillies, or jaggery,[1] or salt even? The house is empty. But there is always something for the thief to find. They creep in while I am away in the jungle; they see the little ones whom I have fed, the little ones who laughed and called me "Appochchi"[2] when I brought them fruits and honeycomb from the jungle. They creep in like the hooded snake, and steal them away from me. Aiyo! aiyo! The little ones laugh to go.'

Punchi Menika rushed forward, threw herself at Silindu's feet, which she touched and caressed with her hands. She struck the ground several times with her forehead, crying and wailing:

'Appochchi! Appochchi! Will you kill me with your words? I will never leave you nor my sister.'

Babun turned upon her:

'Are the words in the jungle nothing then? Did you lie to me when you said you would come to my house? They are right then when they say that women's words are lies – in the morning one thing, at night another. Did I not tell you that I cannot be without you? Aiyo! You told me there under the cassia-tree that you would come to me and cook my rice. And in the evening I am homeless and without you! I shall go now into the jungle and hang myself.'

---

[1] Native sugar made from the kitul palm.   [2] Father.

Babun moved away, but Karlinahami caught hold of his hand and pulled him back. Punchi Menika threw herself on the ground again in front of Silindu.

'Appochchi! it is true: I said I would go to him. Do not kill me with bitter words. I must go: I cannot be without him. I gave my word: what can I do?'

Punchi Menika crouched down at Silindu's feet. He sat very still for a little while, and then began in a low, moaning voice:

'Did I not often tell you of the devils of the trees that lurk for you by the way? I have stood by you against them in the day: I have held you in my arms when they howled about the house at night. I told you that the place is evil, and evil comes from it. They lie in the shadows of the trees, and cast spells on you as you pass. And now one has got you, and you laugh to go from me. They sit in the trees among the grey monkeys and laugh at me as I pass in the morning: they howl at me among the jackals as I come back in the evening. They take all from me, and the house is very empty.'

'Appochchi! the devils are not taking me. I shall not leave you; when you come from the jungle I shall be here with my sister. But the man has called to me and I must go to him. The cub does not always remain in the cave by the father's side: her time comes, and she hears her mate call from the neighbouring rocks: she leaves her father's cave for another's. But, Appochchi, she will still look out for the old leopard when he returns: she will live very close to him'.

'Aiyo! aiyo! the house will be empty.'

'The doe cannot always stay with the herd. She hears the call of the buck, and they fly together into the jungle.'

'The house is empty. There is no use for me to live now.'

Karlinahami, who had been growing more and more impatient, here broke in:

'Are you mad, brother? The child is a woman now, and it is time to give her to a man. Is she to die childless because she has a father? There is no need for her even to leave the compound. There is room for Babun to make himself a house here.'

Babun eagerly seized upon this suggestion. He assured Silindu that he had no intention of taking Punchi Menika out of the compound. Punchi Menika, still crouching at his feet, told her father that she would never leave him.

It was eventually arranged that for the present Babun should live in the house while he put up another house for himself and Punchi Menika. Silindu took no part in the discussion. After Karlinahami intervened, he became silent: there was nothing for him to do or to say which could help him: it was only one more of the evils which inevitably came upon him. The talk died down: the others went into the house to prepare the evening meal. He sat on under the mustard-tree, staring at the outline of the trees against the starlit sky. The silence of the jungle settled down upon the compound. Punchi Menika brought him his food. She tried to comfort him, to get him to come into the house, but for once she could not rouse him. He sat in the compound through the night, staring into the darkness, and muttering from time to time, 'Aiyo, the house is empty!'

CHAPTER V

BABUN put up a new hut in Silindu's compound, and three weeks after he left his brother-in-law, he and Punchi Menika began to live together in it. It was the beginning of a far greater prosperity for the family. Babun worked hard: he cleared the chena and watched it well: his crop was always the best in the village, and the produce went with Silindu's into a barn which served in common for the whole compound.

Silindu did not again refer to Punchi Menika's leaving him. He seemed hardly to be aware of Babun's existence in the compound: he very rarely addressed a word to him. In fact, he now scarcely ever spoke to any one except Hinnihami. When he came back to the compound from the jungle or from the chenas, he never went into the new hut, where Punchi Menika lived: he never called her to him as he had been used to do. If she came out in the evenings to sit with him and speak with him, he answered her questions; but he no longer poured out to her everything that was in his mind, as he still did to Hinnihami. It seemed as if he were unable to share her with another.

And Punchi Menika altered. Her blind love for her father and her sister remained, but it was swamped by a fierce attachment to Babun. She felt the barrier which had grown up and separated her from Silindu, and in a less degree from Hinnihami. And as her life became different, she lost some of the wildness which had before belonged to her. She began to lead a life more like the other village women. She no longer went to, or worked in, the chena; the jungle began to lose its hold on her. She had listened from the time when she first began to understand anything to the tales of her father, and imperceptibly his views of life had become hers: she and he were only two out of the countless animals which wander through the jungle, continually beset by hunger and fear. But as she became more and more separated from him and attached to Babun, this view of life – always vague and unconsciously held – became vaguer and dimmer. The simplicity of Babun reacted upon her: she became the man's woman, the cook of his food, the cleaner of his house, and bearer of his children.

There had always been considerable difference in character between Hinnihami and Punchi Menika. There was very little of her sister's gentleness in Hinnihami. There was, added to the strangeness and wildness which she derived from Silindu, a violence of feeling far greater than his. You could see this in her eyes, which gradually lost the melancholy of childhood, and glowed with a fierce, startled look through the long black hair, which hung in disorder about her pale brown face. The village women, who never tired of following Nanchohami's lead in jeering at Karlinahami and Punchi Menika, soon learned to respect the passionate anger which it was so easy to rouse in Hinnihami.

And the passion of her anger was equalled by the passion of her attachment to Silindu and Punchi Menika. The women soon learned that it was as dangerous to abuse in her presence her father or her sister, as to risk a gibe at the girl herself. It was always remembered in the village how, when Angohami once, worked up by the bitterness of her own tongue, raised her hand against Punchi Menika, Hinnihami, then a child of eight, had seized the baby which the woman was carrying on her hip and flung it into the tank water.

Hinnihami had taken no part in the discussion about her sister's marriage. But when Babun took Punchi Menika to live with him in the hut which he had built, she felt an instinctive dislike towards him, a feeling that she was being robbed of something. Her father and her sister were everything to her: for she had never felt for Karlinahami the blind affection which she felt for them. She could not understand, therefore, how Punchi Menika could turn from them to this man whom she had scarcely known the day before.

She saw and understood her father's anger and unhappiness, but she could not turn against her sister. Something had happened which she did not understand: 'an evil had come out of the jungle,' as such evils come. If any one could be blamed, it was the stranger Babun; but as her sister desired to go to him, she put on one side her own feelings of anger against him. She watched in silence the new house being put up, and she watched in silence Puñchi Menika leave the old hut for the new. She felt as if she were losing somthing; that her sister was going away from her, and that her life had greatly altered. She turned with an increasing passion of attachment to her father; she refused to allow Karlinahami to cook his food for him; if he went out alone in the jungle, she would sit for hours in the compound watching the path by which she knew he would return; and whenever he would allow her, she followed him on his expeditions.

The marriage of Punchi Menika and Babun created a great sensation in the village. The headman and his wife did not at first hide their anger, and the thought that they had been crossed was not unpleasant to many of the villagers. Moreover, Babun was liked, and in many ways respected. The contempt in which the veddas had been held could no longer be shown towards a compound where he had married and where he lived. The compound was no longer avoided; the men entered it now to see Babun, and the women began to come and gossip with Punchi Menika.

It was not in Babehami's nature to remain long openly an enemy of any one. His cunning mind was inclined to, and suited for, intrigue. He understood how much easier – and more enjoyable – it is to harm your enemy, if he thinks that you are his friend, rather than if he knows you are his enemy. He was, however, too angry with Babun for any open reconciliation. He hid his anger; and though he never went into Babun's compound, nor Babun into his, when they met in the village paths, they spoke to one another as if there was nothing between them. But he often thought over the reckoning which he was determined one day to have; and it was Silindu and his family who, he made up his mind, would feel it most heavily. He was a man who never forgot what he considered a wrong done him. He could wait long to repay a real or imaginary injury: the repayment might be made in many diverse ways, but until it was repaid with interest his mind was unsatisfied.

As time passed Silindu's family began again to enter into the ordinary village life. It was natural, therefore, that the hesitation which the villager might have felt to take a wife from the family died down before Babun's example. People who live in towns can hardly realise how persistent and violent are the desires of those who live in villages like Beddagama. In many ways, and in this beyond all others, they are very near to the animals; in fact, in this they are more brutal and uncontrolled than the brutes; that, while the animals have their seasons, man alone is perpetually dominated by his desires.

Hinnihami, both in face and form, was more desirable than any of the other women. It was about a year after Babun and Punchi Menika began to live together that proposals began to be made about her. There lived in one of the huts with his old mother, a man called Punchirala. He was a tall, thin, dark man, badly afflicted with parangi. The naturally crafty look of his face had been intensified by an accident. When a young man he had been attacked by a bear, which met him crawling under the bushes in search of a hive of wild bees which he had heard in the jungle. The bear mauled him, and had left the marks of its teeth and claws upon his cheeks and forehead, and partially destroyed his right eye. The drooping lid of the injured eye gave him the appearance of perpetually and cunningly winking. He had some reputation in the village as a vederala or doctor, and also a dealer in spells. The result of his quarrel with his brother had made him feared and respected. They had cultivated a chena in common, and a dispute had arisen over the division of the produce. Punchirala considered himself to have been swindled. He went out into the jungle and collected certain herbs, leaves, and fruit. He put them in a cocoanut shell together with a lime, and placed them at night in the corner of his brother's compound. The next morning his brother was found to be lying unable to speak or move. The wife and mother came and begged Punchirala to remove the spell. He denied all knowledge of the matter, and in three days his brother died. The brother's share of the chena produce was handed over to Punchirala, as no one else was inclined to run the risk of the curse which appeared to attach to it.

Punchirala was about thirty-eight years old. The woman who had lived with him had died about a year previously, and the marriage of Babun had directed his attention towards Hinnihami. His first proposals were made to the girl herself. He was astonished by the fury with which they were rejected, but he was not discouraged. He watched for his opportunity; and some days later, when Hinnihami was not there, he went to Silindu's compound. He found Silindu sitting in the shadow of the hut.

'I heard,' he said to him, 'that you have an ulcer in your foot. Let me see. Aiyo! caused by a bad thorn! Here are some leaves. I brought them with me. They will do it good.'

Silindu had been unable to walk for some days owing to the swelling and pain. He was very glad to show the foot to the vederala. Punchirala sat down to examine it, and Karlinahami and Babun came out to see what was going on. This was exactly what Punchirala wanted. He heated the leaves by putting them in hot water, which he made Karlinahami fetch. He tied them on with much ceremony, and then the whole party squatted down to talk.

'This medicine I learned from my father,' he told them. 'It is of great power. It will draw the evil and the heat out of the foot into the leaves, and to-morrow you will be able to walk.'

The power of medicine and spells was a subject which never failed to appeal to Karlinahami.

'They say your father was a great man, and that in those days people came to the village from all sides for his medicine.'

'Ah, but he was a great man, and I have all my knowledge from him. Now the Government builds hospitals, and makes people go to them, and gives them Government medicine, which is useless. And so our work is taken from us, and people die of these foreign medicines. But my father was a great man. He knew of many charms: one which would bring any woman to a man. There is a tale about that charm. In those days there lived a

Korala Mahatmaya by the sea, a big-bellied man, a great lover of women. Down the coast, beyond his village, was a village in which only Malay people live. The Malay women are before all others in beauty, very fair, with eyes shaped like pomegranate seeds. They are Mohammedan people, and no Sinhalese can approach their women; for the men are very jealous, and also strong and fearless. They are bad men. The Korala Mahatmaya used to go to the village on Government work, and every time he walked through the street, and saw the women peeping at him from the doorways – and he saw their eyes shaped like pomegranate seeds, shining beneath the cloths which covered their head – he was very troubled, and longed to have a Malay woman. At last he could bear it no longer: so he lay down in his house, and sent a message to my father to say that he was very ill, and that he should come to him at once. Then my father went three days' journey to the Korala's house; and, when he came there, the Korala Mahatmaya sent all the women out of the house, and he made my father sit down by his side, and he said to him, "Vederala, I am very ill. I cannot sleep: I have a great desire day and night in me for a woman from the Malay village along the coast. I can get no pleasure from my own women. But if I be seen even talking to a Malay woman, the men of the village would rise and beat me to death. The desire is killing me. Now you, I know, have great skill in charms. You must make me one therefore which will bring a Malay woman to me to a place of which I will tell you." Then my father said, "Hamadoru! I dare not do this. For I must go and make the charm in the compound of the girl's house. And I know these Malay people: they are very bad men. If they catch me there, they will kill me." But the Korala Mahatmaya said, "There is no need to fear. There is a house at the end of the village standing somewhat apart from the others. There lives in it a young girl, unmarried, the daughter of Tuwan Abdid. I will take you there on a moonless night, and you will make the charm there. And if the next night the girl comes to me, I will give you £5."[1] Then my

---

[1] Colloquially used for 50 rupees.

father thought, "If I refuse the Korala Mahatmaya, he will be angry, and put me into trouble, and ruin me; and if I consent to his wish I will gain £5, which is much money, and possibly a beating from the Malay men. It is better to risk the beating." So he agreed to make the charm on a moonless night. Then the Korala Mahatmaya gave out that he was very ill, and that my father was treating him. And for three days my father lived in the house, preparing the charm. On the fourth day the Korala Mahatmaya and my father – taking cold cooked rice with them – set out from the house, saying they were going to my father's village for the treatment of the Korala with medicines in my father's house. But after leaving the village they turned aside from the path, and went secretly through the jungle to a cave near the Malay village. The cave was hidden in thick jungle, and they lay there through the day. When it was night and very dark they crept out, and the Korala showed the house to my father. My father stood in the garden of the house, and made the charm, and buried it in the earth of the garden, and returned to the cave with the Korala Mahatmaya. All through the next day they lay in the cave, and ate only the cold rice, and the Korala Mahatmaya talked much of the Malay women, and their eyes, which were shaped like pomegranate seeds. And in the evening, at the time when the women go to draw water, the girl came to the cave, and the Korala Mahatmaya enjoyed her. Then he sent her away, and he called my father who was sitting outside in the jungle, and told him that the girl was cross-eyed and ugly, and not worth £5, but at the most ten rupees. He gave my father ten rupees, and told him he would give the other forty some other time – but the money was never paid. Next day they went back to the Korala's house, and told a tale how the Korala Mahatmaya had got well on the way to my faher's village, and so they had returned at once. But the girl had seen the Korala Mahatmaya in the village, and she recognised his black face and big belly, and she told her mother how she had been charmed to go to the cave. The mother told the Malay men, and they were very angry. Next time that the Korala Mahatmaya went to their village, they set upon him, and beat him with clubs and sticks until he nearly died. Then they put him in a bullock-cart, and tied his hands together above his head to the hood of the cart, and took him twelve miles into Kamburupitiya, to the Agent Hamadoru, and said that they had caught the Korala Mahat-maya with a bag on his back stealing salt. And there was a great case, and the magistrate Hamadoru believed the story of the Korala Mahatmaya, who had many witnesses to show that on the very day on which the girl said she had gone to the cave they had seen him on the road to my father's village. So the Malay men all were sent to prison; but my father got a great name; for all the country, except the magistrate Hamadoru, knew of the charm by which he had brought the girl to the fat Korala Mahatmaya in the cave.'

'Did your father teach you the making of the charm?' asked Karlinahami.

'Am I not the vederala and the son of a vederala? The learning of the father is handed down to the son.'

'Yes, I remember hearing my mother speak of him: there was no one in the district, she said, so skilled in charms and medicines as your father.'

'Yes, he knew many things which other vederalas know nothing of. He had a charm by which devils are charmed to become the servants of the charmer. He learnt it from a man of Sinhala,[1] who lived long ago in the neighbouring village. This man was called Tikiri Banda, and he wanted to marry the daughter of the headman. The headman refused to give her, and Tikiri Banda being very angry put a charm upon a devil which lived in a banian-tree. And the devil took a snake in his hand and touched the headman with it on the back as he passed under the tree in the dusk, and the headman's back was bent into a bow for the rest of his days.'

'Was that the village called Bogama?' asked Silindu, who had listened with interest. 'Where the nuga-trees[2] now stand in the jungle to the south? The last house was abandoned when I was a boy, but the devil still dances beneath the nuga-trees.'

'Yes, it was Bogama. It was a village like this in my father's

---

[1] Kandyan district.   [2] The banian-tree.

time, and in your father's time. I can myself remember houses there near the nuga-trees.'

'Of course,' said Karlinahami. 'Podi Sinho's wife Angohami came from there. Aiyo! when the jungle comes in, how things are forgotten!'

'Well, well,' said the vederala, 'the devils still dance under the trees, though the men have gone. The chena crops were bad, and every year the fever came; it is the same now in this village. The old medicines of the vederalas are no longer used, but people go to the towns and hospitals for these foreign medicines. But they die very quickly, and where there was a village there are only trees and devils!'

The little group was silent for a while; nothing could be heard but the sigh of the wind among the trees for miles around them. Then the vederala began to speak again:

'Yes, that was a wonderful charm. The headman walked bow-backed for the rest of his life because he would not give the girl. Aiyo! it is always the women who bring trouble to us men, and yet what can a man do? A man without a wife, they say, is only half a man. There is no comfort in a house where there is no woman to cook the meal.'

'There is no need to use your charm, vederala,' said Karlinahami, 'if you want one for yourself.'

'There is only one unmarried woman in the village now,' said the vederala, 'and she is Silindu's daughter.'

An uncomfortable silence fell upon the listeners. Karlinahami and Babun looked at Silindu, who remained silent, his eyes fixed upon the ground. The vederala's intentions were very clear, and the point of his previous stories very obvious now. Punchirala turned to Karlinahami:

'I was thinking but yesterday that it is time that the girl was given in marriage. Babun here has taken her twin sister, and it is wrong that a woman should live alone.'

'It is not for me to give the girl. She is her father's daughter.'

Silindu's face showed his distress. The vederala was a dangerous man to offend, but too much was being asked of him. He began in a low voice:

'The girl is too young; she has not flowered yet.'

Punchirala laughed.

'Did you bring the girl up or only filth, as the saying is? They are called twins, but the one has been married a year and the other has not flowered yet!'

'Vederala! I would give the girl, but she is unwilling. She told me last night that you had spoken to her. She is of the jungle, wild, not fit for your house. She was very frightened and angry.'

For a moment Punchirala was disconcerted that his rebuff was known. But anger came to his rescue.

'Am I to ask the girl then when I want a wife? Can the father not give his child? So the child is angry, and the father obeys! Ohé! strange customs spring up! You are a fool, Silindu. If you tell the child to obey, there is no more to be said.'

'The girl is a wild thing, I tell you. I cannot give her against her will.'

The vederala got up. He smiled at Silindu, who watched him anxiously.

'You will not give the girl, Silindu?'

'I cannot, I cannot.'

'You will not give her? Remember the man of Sinhala, who taught my father.'

'Aiyo! how can I do this?'

'And the headman of Bogama, and the devil that still dances beneath the trees.'

Silindu's face worked with excitement.

'Ask anything else of me, vederala. I cannot do this, I cannot do this.'

Punchirala walked away. The others watched him in silence. When he got to the fence of the compound, he turned round and smiled at them again.

'And don't forget,' he called out, 'to tell the girl about the Malay girl who came to the Korala Mahatmaya in the cave. A black-faced man and big-bellied, but she came, she came. I am an ugly man, and the bear's claws have made me uglier; a poor bed-fellow for a girl! And so was he, black as a Tamil, and a great belly swaying as he walked. But she came to the cave, to the calling of my father's charm. Oh yes, she came, she came.'

Punchirala walked away chuckling. Silindu was trembling with excitement and fear. Karlinahami burst out into a wail of despair.

'Aiyo! what will become of us, brother? He is a bad man, a bad man; very cunning and clever. There is no protection against his charms. He will bring evil and disease upon the house: he will make devils enter us. What have you done? What have you done? Aiyo!'

Babun was not as excited as the other two, but he was very serious.

'It would perhaps have been better to give him the girl,' he said. 'The man is not a bad man if you do not cross him, and the girl is of age to marry. Even the bravest man does not go down the path where a devil lives.'

'Only the fool struggles against the stronger,' said Karlinahami. 'What the vederala says is medicine, is medicine. It is not too late, brother, to undo the evil. To whom else in the village can you give the girl?'

Silindu turned upon them in his anger and fear:

'Have you too joined to plague me? Evils come upon a man: it is fate. What can I do? The girl is unwilling: am I to throw away the kurakkan when the rice is already stolen? Am I to help the thief to plunder my house? I am a poor man, and the evil has come upon me; I can do nothing against it. His devils will enter me, and I shall waste away. But as for the child, what else is left to me? I will not force her to go to this son of a ——. Go into the house, woman, and cry there; and you, Babun, is it not enough that you have stolen from me one child that now you should join with this dog to steal the other from me?'

The other two were frightened by this outburst of Silindu; they saw that to argue with him would only increase his excitement. They left him. He remained squatting in the compound, and as his anger died down fear possessed him utterly. He had no doubt of the powers of Punchirala over him: he knew that he had delivered himself into his power, and the power of the devils that surrounded him. He had no thought of resistance in such a case. The terrible sense of a blank wall of fate, against which a man may hurl himself in vain, was upon him. He sat terrified and crushed by the inevitableness of the evil which must be. When Hinnihami returned, he told her what had happened, and she shared in his terror and despair.

The charms of the vederala did not take long to act upon Silindu. He felt that he was a doomed man, and his mind could think of nothing but the impending evil. The banian-trees of the ruined village of Bogama obsessed his mind: he knew that ruin waited for him there, and yet a horrible desire to see them was always present with him. He could no longer remain in the hut or compound: he wandered through the jungle, fighting against the pull of the desire: his wanderings became a circle, of which the banian-trees were the centre. He tried to go back to his hut, where he felt that there was safety for him, and found himself walking in the opposite direction. Darkness began to settle over the jungle, and the life, which awakes only in its darkness, began to stir. Voices mocked him from the canopy of leaves above him: dim forms moved among the shadows of the trees. Suddenly a blind terror came upon him, and he began to run through the dense jungle. The boughs of the trees lashed him as he ran down the narrow tracks; the thorns tore him like spurs. He lost all sense of direction; vague shapes seemed to follow him in the darkness; enormous forms broke away from the track before him, to crash away among the undergrowth and trees. The throbbing of his heart and throat became unendurable, but still his one idea was to run. As he ran the jungle suddenly became thinner; the thorny undergrowth had given way to more open spaces. Even here it was very dark. He stumbled against the knotted root of a tree; a long, straight, swinging bough struck him in the face; a wild, derisive yell came from above. The blood seemed to rise and drown in his eyes: he felt about vaguely with his hands. He recognised the root-like, stringy trunks of the banian-trees: he heard the cry ring out above his head, and he fell huddled together among the roots of the trees.

Silindu did not hear again the cry of the devil-bird from the tree-tops. He lay unconscious throughout the night. When dawn broke he came to himself stiff and cold. He dragged himself slowly to the hut. There was no necessity to tell the others what had happened. The pale yellow of his skin, his sunken glazed eyes, his shivering body told them that Punchirala's charms had already begun their work, and his devils had already entered Silindu. He lay down on a mat within the hut to wait for the slow sapping of his life by the spell.

For the next two days Silindu lay in the hut, very slowly letting go his hold of life. A kind of coma was upon him, as he felt life gradually slipping from his body. From time to time the women began a shrill wail in the compound. Babun went to expostulate with Punchirala; but the vederala, after listening with a malignant smile, replied that he knew nothing, and could do nothing, in the matter. Babun returned to lounge moodily about the compound.

On the second day Karlinahami determined in despair to go herself to the vederala. She found him sitting in his compound.

'You have come about your brother, no doubt. But I can do nothing; I'm only a poor vederala. There is the Government hospital in Kamburupitiya, and a Mahatmaya in trousers, a drinker of arrack, a clever man; he will give you Government medicines free of charge – just a fanam or two for the peon who stands by the door. You should take your brother there. It is only three days' journey.'

'Vederala! my brother lies in the hut dying. He has covered his head with his cloth, and he will neither eat nor speak. Life is slipping from him.'

'The doctor Mahatmaya will say it is the fever. He will give you a bottle of fever mixture – free of charge. A clever man, the doctor Mahatmaya. Yes, you should take him to the hospital and get the medicine – free of charge. It is a good medicine, though unpleasant to the taste, they tell me.'

'Aiyo! what is the good of going to the hospital? Why do you talk like that, vederala? You are laughing at me. We know that it is the devils that have entered my brother, and that you alone have power to save him.'

'Devils! what do I know of devils? No, they tell me the doctor

Mahatmaya keeps no medicine in the hospital against devils. The Government says there are no devils. Surely it is fever, or fire-fever,[1] or dysentery. It is for these that they give Government medicine. No, it is no good going to the hospital for devils.'

'Vederala! I have brought you kurakkan here; it is all I have. And I will talk to the girl for you, yes, and to my brother if he gets well. But take the spell from him, vederala; take the spell from him, I pray you.'

'I know nothing of spells. I am a poor village vederala with a little knowledge of roots and leaves and fruits, which my father taught me.'

'Vederala, you yourself told us of the charms and spells. Your skill is known. Charm the devil to leave my brother. He meant no harm; he is a strange man – you know that, vederala. He never meant to injure you. The girl will come to you, I will see to that – only take the spell from my brother.'

Punchirala sat and looked at Karlinahami, smiling, for a little while. Then he said, 'Is the woman mad too? What do I know of charms and spells? I can work no charm on your brother. But I have some little knowledge of devils – my father taught me. Well, well, let me think now. If a devil has entered the man, and is slowly taking his life from him, perhaps there is a way. Let me think. Do you know the village of Beragama?'

'No, vederala, no. I have heard of it, but I do not know it.'

'Well, it lies over there to the east, five days' journey through the jungle, beyond Maha Potana and the River of Jewels. Do you think you could take your brother there?'

'Yes, vederala, we could go there.'

'There is a great temple there, and the great Beragama deviyo[2] lives in it. He is a Tamil god, so they say; but Sinhalese kapuralas[3] serve him in the temple. My father used to say that he is a very great god. His power is over the jungle, and the devils who live in it. The devils of the trees obey him, for his anger is terrible. If a devil has entered a man, and is harming him, and

---

[1] Typhoid.
[2] Deviyo used of a god.
[3] Kapuralas are persons who perform various services in temples.

taking his life from him, the man should make a vow to the god, so my father used to say. Then he should go to the temple at Beragama at the time of the great festival, and roll in the dust round the temple three times every day, and call upon the god in a loud voice to free him from the devil. And perhaps, if he call loud enough, the god will hear him and order the devil to leave him. Then the devil will be afraid of the god's power, and will leave the man, who will be freed from the evil. Now the great festival falls on the day of the next full moon. Perhaps if your brother makes a vow to the Beragama deviyo, and goes to the great festival, the devil will be driven out by the god. You and the girl might take him there; and perhaps I will go too, for I have made a vow myself.'

Karlinahami fell at the vederala's feet, salaaming and whimpering blessings on him. Then she hurried home. It took a long time to make Silindu understand that there was hope for him. At first he would not listen to their entreaties and exhortations. At last, when he was prevailed upon to believe that it was Punchirala himself who had suggested the remedy, some spirit to fight for life seemed to creep into him. He took some food for the first time, and sat listening to the plans for the pilgrimage. It was decided that they should start on the next day, and that Babun should accompany them.

The next day the pilgrims set out on a journey which, with the enfeebled Silindu, would they knew take them at least six days. Their road the whole way led them through thick jungle; villages were few, and what there were consisted only of a few squalid huts. The only village of any size through which they were to pass was Maha Potana, an agricultural village, one day's journey from Beragama, which had sprung up around a vast tank restored by Government. They carried their food with them, and slept at night on the bare earth under bushes or trees. Every day they trudged, straggling along in single file, from seven to eleven in the morning, and from three to six in the evening. Silindu was dazed and weak, and often had to be helped along by Babun. The women carried large bundles of food and chatties,[1] wrapped

---

[1] Earthenware pots.

up in cloths, upon their heads. It was the hottest time of the year, when the jungle is withered with drought, the grass has died down, the earth is caked and cracked with heat; the trees along the paths and road are white with dust. The pools had dried up, and the little streams were now mere channels of gleaming sand. Often they had to go all day without finding a pool or a well with water in it. For twelve hours every day the sun beat down upon them fiercely; the quivering heat from the white roads beat up into their faces and eyes; the wind swept them with its burning gusts and eddies of dust. Their feet were torn by the thorns, and swollen and blistered by the hot roads. As Hinnihami followed hour after hour along the white track, which for ever coiled out before her into the walls of dusty trees, the old song, which Karlinahami had sung to them when they were children, continually was in her mind, and she sang as she walked:

> 'Our women's feet are weary, but the day
> Must end somewhere for the followers in the way.

Two days' journey from Beddagama they joined a larger and more frequented track. Here they continually met little bands of pilgrims bound for the same destination as themselves. The majority of them were Tamils, Hindus from India, from the tea estates, and from the north and east of the island; strange-looking men, such as Hinnihami had never seen before; very dark, with bodies naked to the waist; with lines of white and red paint on their shoulders, their foreheads smeared with ashes, and the mark of God's eye between their eyebrows. They wore clothes of fine white cotton, caught up between the legs, and they carried brass bowls and brass tongs. Their women, heavy and sullen-looking, followed, carrying bundles and children.

There were, however, also little bands of Buddhists, Sinhalese like themselves and to one of these bands they attached themselves. Four of them were a family from a village only twenty miles north of Beddagama, and jungle people like themselves. They were taking a blind child to see whether, if they called upon the god, he would hear them and give him sight. There were a fisher and his wife from the coast; they were childless, and the woman had vowed to go to the festival and touch the heel of the kapurala, in order that the god might remove from her the curse of barrenness. Last, there was an old man, a trader from a large and distant village of another district; he wore immense spectacles, and all day long he walked reading or chanting from a large Sinhalese religious book, which he carried open in his hand. The rest of the party did not understand a word of what he read, but they felt that he was acquiring merit, and that they would share a little of it. He had been brought up in a Buddhist temple, and at night after the evening meal he gathered the little party round him and preached to them, or read to them, by the light of the camp-fire, how they should live in order to acquire merit in this life. And at the appropriate places they all cried out together, 'Sadhu! sadhu!' or he made them all repeat together aloud the sil or rules; and as their voices rose and fell in the stillness of the night air, Karlinahami's face shone with ecstasy, and a sense of well-being and quiet, strange to her, stole over Hinnihami. Even in Silindu there came a change; he joined in the chant:

Búddhun sáránam gáchchāmí,'

with which they began and ended the day; he became less hopeless and sullen, and the look of fear began to leave his eyes. In the evenings, when the air grew cool and gentle after the pitiless heat and wind of the day; as they sat around the fire by the roadside; and the great trees rose black behind them into the night; and the stars blazed above them between the leaves; and up and down the road twinkled the fires of other pilgrims, and the air was sweet with the smell of burning wood and the hum of voices; and the vast stillness of the jungle folded them round on every side; and they listened to the strange words, but half understood, of the Lord Buddha, and how he attained to Nirvana; – then the sufferings of the day were forgotten, and a feeling stole over them of peace and holiness and merit acquired.

And one evening, at Babun's suggestion, Karlinahami told them a story which had always been a favourite with the village women. At first the old man with the book and spectacles showed signs of being offended at this usurpation; but he was soothed by their saying that they did not want to tire him, and by their asking him to read to them again after the story was finished. In the end he was an absorbed listener as Karlinahami told the following story:[1]

'The Lord Buddha, in one of his previous lives, met a young girl carrying kunji[2] to her father, who was ploughing in the field. And when he saw her he thought, "The maiden is fair. If she is unmarried she would make me a fit wife." And she thought when she saw him, "If such a one took me to wife, I would bring fortune to my family." And he said to her, "What is your name?" Her name was Amara Devi, which means "undying," so she replied, "Sir, my name is that which never was, is, nor will be in this world." "Nothing," he said, "born in this world is undying. Is your name Amara?" She answered, "Yes, sir." Then the Buddha said, "To whom are you taking the kunji?" "To the first god." "You are taking it to your father?" "Yes, sir." "What is your father doing?" "He makes one into two." "To make one into two is to plough. Where is your father ploughing?" "He ploughs in that place from which no man returns." "No man returns from the grave. Is he ploughing near the burial-ground?" "Yes, sir." Then Amara Devi offered the Buddha kunji to drink, and he accepted it, and he thought to himself, "If the maiden gives me the kunji without first washing the pot, I will leave her at once." But Amara Devi washed the pot first, and then gave the kunji. The Buddha drank the kunji, and said, "Friend, where is your house that I may go to it?" And Amara Devi answered, "Go by this path until you come to a boutique where they sell balls of rice and sugar; go on until you come to another where they sell kunji. From there you will see a flamboyant-tree in full blossom. At that tree take the path towards the hand with which you eat rice.[3] That is the way to my father's house." And the Buddha went as Amara Devi had directed him, and found the

[1] This story is taken from the Ummaga Jataka.
[2] A sort of rice gruel.
[3] The 'hand with which you eat rice' is a common expression for the right hand, the left hand being used for an unmentionable purpose.

house, and went in. Amara Devi's mother was in the house, and she welcomed the Buddha, and made him sit down. And he, seeing the poverty of the house, said, "Mother, I am a tailor. Have you anything for me to sew?" And she said, "Son, there are clothes and pillows to mend, but I have no money to pay for the mending." Then he replied, "There is no need of money; bring them for me to mend." So the Lord Buddha sat and mended the torn clothes and pillows; and in the evening Amara Devi came back from the fields carrying a bundle of firewood on her head, and a sheaf of jungle leaves in the folds of her cloth. And Buddha lived in the house some days in order to learn the behaviour of the girl. At the end of three days he gave her half a seer[1] of rice, and said, "Amara Devi, cook for me kunji, boiled rice, and cakes." She never thought to say, "How can I cook so much out of half a seer of rice?" but was ready to do as she was told. She cleaned the rice, boiled the whole grains, made kunji from the broken grains, and cakes from the dust. She offered the kunji to the Buddha, and he took a mouthful and tasted the delight of its sweetness, but to try her he spat it out on the ground, and said, "Friend, since you do not know how to cook, why do you waste my rice?" Amara Devi took no offence, but offered him the cakes, saying, "Friend, if the kunji does not please you, will you eat of the cakes?" And the Buddha did the same with the cakes. Then Amara Devi offered him the rice, and again he spat out the rice, and pretended to be very angry, and smeared the food upon her head and body, and made her stand in the sun before the door. The girl showed no anger, but went out and stood in the sun. Then the Buddha said, "Amara Devi, friend, come here," and she came to him, and he took her as his wife, and lived with her in the city in the gatekeeper's house. And she still thought he was a tailor, and one day he sent two men to her with a thousand gold pieces to try her. The men took the gold pieces, and with them tempted her, but she said, "These thousand gold pieces are unworthy to wash my husband's feet." And three times she was tempted, and at last he told them to bring her to him by force. So

---

[1] A small measure.

they brought her to him by force, and when she came into his
presence she did not know him, for he sat in state in his robes,
but she smiled and wept when she looked at him. The Buddha
asked her why she smiled and wept, and she said, "Lord, I smiled
with joy to see your divine splendour and the merit acquired by
you in innumerable births; but when I thought that in this birth
you might by some evil act, such as this, by seducing another's
wife, earn the pains of death, I wept for love of you." Then the
Buddha sent her back to the house of the gatekeeper, and he told
the king and queen that he had found a princess for his wife. And
the queen gave jewels and gold ornaments to Amara Devi, and
she was taken in a great chariot to the house of the Buddha, and
from that day she lived happily with him as his wife.'

The other pilgrims, except the fisher, who had fallen asleep,
were delighted with Karlinahami's story, and they wanted her to
tell them another. But she was afraid to offend the old man
again, so she refused. The old man read to them a while, and
gradually, one after the other, they dropped off to sleep. And in
the morning they started off again down the long white road;
and at midday, when they were hot and footsore, the wall of
jungle before them parted suddenly, and they came out into a
great fertile plain. The green rice-fields stretched out before
them, dotted over with watch-huts and clumps of cocoanut-trees
and red-roofed houses, and the immense white domes of dagobas gleaming in the sun. Beyond shone the pleasant sheet of
water through which the jungle had yielded the smiling plain;
the dead trees still stood up gaunt and black from its surface;
great white birds sat upon the black branches, or flapped lazily
over the water with wild, hoarse cries; its bosom was starred and
dappled with pink lotus-flowers. And beyond again lay the long
dark stretch of jungle, out of which, far away to the north,
towered into the fiery sky the line of dim blue hills. It was the
tank and village of Maha Potana; and when the weary band of
pilgrims suddenly saw the monotony of the trees and of the
parched jungle give place to the water, and the green fields, and
the white dagobas, the shrines built by kings long ago to hold the
relics of the Lord Buddha, they raised their hands, salaaming,

and cried aloud, 'Sadhu! Sadhu!'[1]

They picked lotus-flowers, and went to the great dagoba, which is called after an ancient king, and laid the flowers upon the shrine as an offering, and walked three times around, crying, 'Sadhu! Sadhu!' and thus acquired merit. Then they went into the bazaar which was crowded with pilgrims, Hindus and Buddhists, and Indian fakirs and Moormen. Innumerable bullock-carts stood on the road and paths and open spaces, and the air rang with the bells of the bulls, which lazily fed upon the great bundles of straw tied to the carts.

And the old man, who had noted the poverty of Silindu and his family, bought them rice and curry and plantains. So they sat under the shade of a great bo-tree, and ate a meal such as Hinnihami had never eaten before. Her eyes wandered vacantly from thing to thing; she was dazed by the crowd perpetually wandering to and fro, by the confused din of talking people, of coughing cattle, and jangling bells. In the evening they went to another dagoba, and then returned to the bo-tree and lighted their fire. All about them were other little fires, around which sat groups, like themselves, of pilgrims eating the evening meal. They ate rice again and cakes, and Hinnihami grew heavy with sleepiness. A great peace came upon her as she heard Karlinahami tell of how she had before come on pilgrimage to the great Buddhist festival at Maha Potana, when the crowds were tens of thousands more. And the old man told of a pilgrimage to the sacred city of Anuradhapura on the great poya day, when hundreds of thousands acquire merit by encircling the shrine; and the merit to be acquired by climbing Adam's Peak, or by visiting the ruined shrines of Situlpahuwa, which the jungle has covered, so that the bears and leopards have made their lairs in the great caves by the side of Buddhas, who lie carved out of rock. The air was heavy with the smell of cooking and the pungent smell of the burning wood; the voice of the old man seemed to come from very far away. She covered her head with a

[1] Sadhu is an exclamation of assent or approval, which people listening to the reading of Banna or Buddhist scriptures repeat at intervals. It is also used by pilgrims at the sight of temples or dagobas.

cloth and lay down on the bare ground. For the first time the bareness and fear and wildness of life had fallen from her; she fell asleep in the peace of well-being, and the merit which she had acquired.

Next morning, to the regret of all, they had to leave the pleasant village and resting-place of Maha Potana, and face again the suffering and weariness of the jungle. For two days their path led them through low thorny jungle, where there was little shelter from the sun. The track became stony and rocky; great boulders of grey lichen-covered rock were strewn among the thick undergrowth; at intervals could be seen enormous rocks towering above the trees. In the afternoon of the first day they caught their first glimpse of the sacred Beragama hill, which rises into three rounded peaks above the village and temple. Next day, towards evening, they had reached the high forest, which, starting from its foot, clothed the hill almost to its peaks.

Then, once again, the jungle parted suddenly, and they stood upon the bank of a great stream. The banks were deep, and enormous trees, kumbuk with its peeling bark and the wild fig-tree, shaded them. The season of drought had narrowed the stream of water, so that it flowed shallow in the centre of the channel, leaving on either side a great stretch of white sand. Up and down stream were innumerable pilgrims, washing from them in the sacred waters the dust of the journey, and the impurities of life, before they entered the village. They followed the example of the other pilgrims, and performed the required ablution; after which they put on clean white clothes, and climbed a path on the opposite bank which led them into the village.

They found themselves in a long, very broad street, on each side of which were boutiques and houses and large buildings — resting-places for the pilgrims. The street was thronged with pilgrims, idling, buying provisions, hurrying to the temple. It was near the time for the procession to start from the temple. The festival lasted fourteen days, and every night the god was taken in procession through the village: it culminated in the great procession of the fourteenth night, which falls when the moon is full; and in the ceremony of the following morning, when the kapurala goes down, accompanied by all the pilgrims, into the bed of the river, and 'cuts the waters' with a golden knife. Silindu and his party arrived in Beragama on the ninth day of the festival, so that they would remain six days in the village, and take part in six processions.

At either end of the broad straight street stood temples. The one at the north end belonged to the Beragama deviyo: the temple or dewala itself was a small, squat, oblong building, above which at one end rose the customary dome-like erection of Hindu temples, on which are fantastically carved the images of gods. Around the temple was an enormous courtyard enclosed by red walls of roughly-baked bricks. Just outside the wall of the courtyard on the east side was another and a smaller temple belonging to the god's lawful wife. At the southern end of the street stood another temple: it was a square, dirty white building without a courtyard, but surrounded on all sides by a verandah, in which, among a litter of broken furniture and odds and ends, lounged and squatted and slept a large number of pilgrims. The only entrance to the shrine itself was through a doorway in the front, which was screened by a large curtain ornamented crudely with the figures of gods and goddesses. No one was allowed to enter behind this curtain except the kapuralas, for the temple belonged to the mistress of the Beragama deviyo.

The solemnity of the pilgrimage was intensified in the minds of Silindu and Karlinahami and the other pilgrims, who were villagers like themselves, by the mystery which surrounds the god. On the road and around the fires at night, in the streets of the village, and in the very courtyard of the temple, they listened to the tales and legends; and believing them all without hesitation or speculation they felt, through their strangeness, far more than they had ever felt with the Buddha of dagobas and vihares, that this god was very near their own lives.

Who was he, this Tamil god, living in the wilderness, whom the Tamils said was Kandeswami, the great Hindu god? These Buddhist villagers felt that they could understand him, he was so near to the devils of the trees and jungles whom they knew so

well. He had once lived upon the centre of the three peaks of the
great hill, ruling over the unbroken forest which stretched below
him, tossing and waving north to the mountains, and south to
the sea. That was why every night throughout the festival a fire
blazed from the peak. But one day, as he sat among the bare
rocks upon the top of the hill and looked down upon the
winding river and the trees which cooled its banks, the wish
came to him to go down and live in the plain beyond the river.
Even in those days he was a Tamil god, so he called to a band of
Tamils who were passing, and asked them to carry him down
across the river. The Tamils answered, 'Lord, we are poor men,
and have travelled far on our way to collect salt in the lagoons by
the seashore. If we stop now, the rain may come and destroy the
salt, and our journey will have been for nothing. We will go on,
therefore, and on our way back we will carry you down, and
place you on the other side of the river, as you desire.' The
Tamils went on their way, and the god was angry at the slight
put upon him. Shortly afterwards a band of Sinhalese came by:
they also were on their way to collect salt in the lagoons. Then
the god called to the Sinhalese, and asked them to carry him
down across the river. The Sinhalese climbed the hill, and carried
the god down, and bore him across the river, and placed him
upon its banks under the shadow of the trees, where now stands
his great temple. Then the god swore that he would no longer be
served by Tamils in his temple, and that he would only have
Sinhalese to perform his ceremonies; and that is why to this day,
though the god is a Tamil god, and the temple a Hindu temple,
the kapuralas are all Buddhists and Sinhalese.

The god, therefore, is of the jungle; a great devil, beneficent
when approached in the right manner and season, whose power
lies for miles upon the desolate jungle surrounding his temple
and hill. A power to swear by, for he will punish for the oath
sworn falsely by his hill; a power who will listen to the vow of
the sick or of the barren woman; a power who can aid us against
the devils which perpetually beset us.[1]

[1] There are two distinct races in Ceylon, Tamils and Sinhalese. Their language,
customs, and religions are different. The Tamils are Dravidians, probably the

It was in this way that the pilgrims regarded the god, and they chose well the time of his festival to approach him. For the god loved a hind, and had made her his mistress, and had placed her in the temple which stood at the southern end of his street. On each of the fourteen nights of his festival the kapuralas entered his shrine, and covering the god in a great black cloth, so that no one should look upon him, carried him out, and placed him upon the back of an elephant. Then the pilgrims called upon the name of the god, and with bowls of blazing camphor upon their heads followed him in procession to his mistress's temple. There the kapuralas, blind-folded, took the god, hidden by the cloth, from the elephant, and carried him up the steps of the temple. Again, the pilgrims shouted the god's name, and women pressed forward to touch the kapurala as he passed, for in this way they escape the curse of barrenness. The kapurala carried the god to his mistress, and then retired. Amid the roar of tomtoms, the jangling of bells, the flaring of great lights, and the passionate shouts of the people, the pilgrims prostrated themselves. Then the kapurala, still blindfolded, again slipped behind the curtain into the shrine, and brought out the god and placed him upon the elephant, and the procession followed him back to his own temple.

Silindu and the others reached the village in the evening, only a little while before the procession started. They therefore made their way at once to the great temple, and took their stand among the pilgrims who crowded the courtyard. They had eaten nothing since the midday meal; they were hungry and dizzy after the long days upon the road. Silindu seemed too dazed and weak to take much notice of what was taking place about him, and he had to be helped along by Babun. Karlinahami was awed and devout: an old pilgrim, she knew the demeanour required of her.

The effect upon Hinnihami was different. Tired and hungry though she was, even the great crowd in the courtyard excited

original inhabitants of India; they are Hindus in religion. The Sinhalese are Aryans, and their religion is Buddhism. The Tamils inhabit the north and east of the island, the Sinhalese the remainder.

her. As each new pilgrim arrived he called aloud upon the god; and the whole crowd took up the cry, which rose and fell around the shrine. She who had before never seen more than forty or fifty people in her life felt the weight and breath of thousands that jostled and pressed her. Her heart beat as, under the flare of the torches, hundreds of arms were raised in supplication, and to the crash of the tomtoms the name of the god thundered through the air. The tears came into her eyes and ran down her cheeks as time after time the roll of the many voices surged about her; and when at last the great moment came, and the kapurala appeared carrying the god under the black cloth, and over the sea of arms the elephant lifted up its trunk and trumpeted as the god was placed upon its back, she stretched out her hands and cried to the god to hear her.

They followed in the rear of the procession, where men roll over and over in the dust, and childless women touch the ground with their forehead between every step, in fulfilment of their vows.

Silindu, with drawn face and vacant eyes, dragged himself along, leaning on Babun: Karlinahami, devout and stolid, raised the ceremonial cry at the due stopping-places. But Hinnihami felt the power of the god in her and over them all: she felt how near he was to them, mysteriously hidden beneath the great cloth which lay upon the elephant's back. She felt again the awe which great trees in darkness and the shadows of the jungle at nightfall roused in her, the mystery of darkness and power, which no one can see. And again and again as the procession halted, and the cry of the multitude rolled back to them, her breath was caught by sobs, and again she lifted her hands to the god and called upon his name. She formulated no prayer to him, she spoke no words of supplication: only in excitement and exaltation of entreaty she cried out the name of the god.

They were too tired that night to go into the shrine of the big temple after the procession and see the ceremony there. They had lost sight of the old man in the crowd, so that they had to make their meal off a little food that they had carried with them. Then, worn out by the journey and excitement, they lay down on the bare ground in the courtyard of the temple.

Next morning Silindu was no better. He seemed weaker and more lifeless: it was clear that the devil had not yet left him. Babun remained with him, while Karlinahami and Hinnihami went down to the river to bathe. The excitement of the previous evening had not died out of the girl, and there was much going on around her to keep it up. The village was a small one, and really consisted of little more than the one street of thirty or forty houses, which were roofed with red tiles and had brown walls of mud. Most of the houses were turned into boutiques during the pilgrimage, and the inhabitants prospered by selling provisions to the pilgrims. When Karlinahami and Hinnihami returned from the river, hundreds filled the street, lounging, strolling, gossiping, and purchasing. Every now and then the crowd would gather more thickly in one quarter, and they would see a pilgrim arrive performing some strange vow. There were some who had run a skewer through their tongue and cheeks; another had thrust through the skin of his back a long stick from which hung bowls of milk. At another time they saw a man, naked except for a dirty loin cloth, his long hair hanging about his face, and a great halo of flowers and branches upon his head; thirty or forty great iron hooks had been put through the skin of his back; to every hook was attached a long cord, and all the cords had been twisted into a rope. Another man held the rope, while the first, bearing with his full weight upon it so that the skin of his back was drawn away from his body, danced around in a circle and shouted and sang.

As Karlinahami and Hinnihami were making their way slowly through the crowd, they suddenly heard a soft voice behind them say:

'Well, mother, has not the hospital cured your brother of his fever?' They turned and saw the smiling face and winking eye of the vederala. Hinnihami shrank away from him behind Karlinahami.

'Vederala,' said Karlinahami, 'I must speak with you. Come away from all these people.'

They pushed through the crowd, and going down a narrow opening between two boutiques found themselves in the strip of quiet forest upon the bank of the river. The vederala squatted down under a tree and began to chew betel. Karlinahami squatted down opposite to him, and Hinnihami tried to hide herself behind her from the eye of the vederala, which seemed to her maliciously to wink at her.

Punchirala leaned round and peered at the girl.

'Well, daughter,' he said, ironically emphasising the word 'daughter,' 'what have you come to the god for? Have you touched the kapurala's foot and prayed for a child? Truly they say he is the god of the barren wife. Chi, chi, she covers her face with her hands. Is the man dead then? What has the widow to do in Beragama? Ohé! now, see. She has come to the god for clothing and food,[1] as they say. May the god give her a man, young and fair and strong, a prince with cattle and land. For the girl is fair, even I, the one-eyed old man, can see that — and the god is a great god.'

'Don't talk this nonsense, vederala,' broke in Karlinahami impatiently. 'You shame the girl and frighten her. The god is a great god, we know that, and as you told me we brought my brother here. Aiyo! the long road and the hot sun. We are burnt as black as Tamils and look at our feet. On the road the strong and healthy fall sick, and the sick man grows weaker. Have you sent my brother here to kill him? He lies now in the temple with no strength in him. Last night we took him in the perahera,[2] and called upon the god to hear us. I pray you, vederala — you are a wise man, and renowned for your knowledge — tell me what wrong have we done. The devil remains; the god has not heard us, nor driven him out.'

'Be patient, mother. This fever is a hard thing to cure. Did I not tell you that even in the hospital there is no medicine against it? And it is hard for a man to find the lucky hour. The gecko[3] calls, and the man starts from the house: the man does not hear the sign; he is saying, "You there bring that along!" and, "You

---

[1] An expression used frequently in stories to mean a husband.
[2] Procession, usually a Sinhalese or Buddhist procession.
[3] Lizard. The chirping cry of the gecko is universally regarded as a warning cry of ill omen.

here, where is the bundle with the kurakkan?" So he starts on the journey in an unlucky hour.'

'We heard no gecko, nor any other bad sign. But we had to start quickly, for the time was short. We had no time to consult an astrologer to find the lucky hour.'

'Yes, perhaps that is it. And it is no easy matter, as I told you, to find a cure for these – fevers.'

'But, vederala, what are we to do now? The man's strength goes from him. Even to take him back the long way to the village will be difficult.'

'Patience, mother, patience. You must call louder to the god nightly until the moon is full. Perhaps even now the devil – the fever – is fighting against him.'

'Aiyo! what help for the cultivator when the flies have sucked the strength from the paddy? He sowed in an unlucky hour, and not even the god can help him. Pity us, vederala. Will you not come with us and look at my brother now?"

'Why should I see your brother?' said the vederala angrily. 'What good can I do? Did I not tell you, woman, that I cannot cure your brother's fever? Where the god fails, can the man succeed? O the minds of these women! They say in the village' – here he looked round and smiled at Hinnihami – 'that even the little one is like an untamed buffalo cow.'

'Do not be angry with me, vederala. You are the only help left for us. We are weary with walking, and in grief. How can the women of the house not raise the cry when the brother and father lies dying within? If I have spoken foolishly, pardon my words.'

Punchirala sat silently looking at Hinnihami. The girl was crying. The memory of the great god, whom she had seen go riding by upon the elephant amid the flames and the shouts, the wild god who ruled over the jungle, and to whom the men crowned with flowers and leaves were now dancing in the street, the god to whom she cried so passionately on the night before, had left her: her excitement and exaltation had died out as she listened to the jeering words of Punchirala. She hated him as she had hated him when he approached her before; but as she listened to him talking to Karlinahami, fear – the fear that she felt for unknown evils – gradually crept upon her. She cried helplessly, and Punchirala smiled at her as he watched her. Karlinahami watched his face expectantly and anxiously.

At last Punchirala began again slowly:

'How the girl cries. And for her father too! I am thinking that there is yet something for you to do. I am a poor vederala, and my powers are small. But there is a man here, a great man, a holy man, who they say is very skilled in medicine and magic, and knows the mind of the god. He is a sanyasi[1] from beyond the sea, from India, and his hair is ten cubits[2] in length. Perhaps if you take Silindu to him, and inquire of him, he will tell you the god's mind. But you must take money for him.'

'Aiyo! what is the use of talking of money to the starving?'

Punchirala fumbled in the fold of his cloth, and drew out his betel-case. From this he took a very dirty rag, in which were a number of copper and silver coins. He made up the sum of ninety-five cents, and handed it over to Karlinahami.

'Here you are then, a rupee. Even the gods require payment. You can pay me three shillings in kurakkan when the crop is reaped. The sanyasi sits behind the little temple under a banian-tree. To-day, when the sun sinks behind the trees of the jungle, take your brother to him and make inquiry.'

Punchirala got up and began walking away, followed by the obeisances and profuse thanks of Karlinahami. The two women hurried back to the temple. They found that the old man and the fisher and his wife had joined Silindu and Babun. The whole party agreed that the only thing to do was to consult the sanyasi. They waited, dozing and talking through the hot afternoon, until the hour fixed by the vederala arrived.

As soon as the sun sank behind the jungle, and the shadow of the trees fell upon the temple courtyard, they went in a body to the banian-trees. They found the sanyasi sitting with his back against the trunk of a tree with a brass bowl by his side. He was unlike any sanyasi whom they had seen before. He had a long black beard reaching below his waist, a big hooked nose, and

[1] A holy man or religious beggar Hindu.   [2] Fifteen feet.

little twinkling black eyes. He wore a long white cotton robe, which was indescribably dirty, and an enormous dirty white turban. As they approached him he unwound the folds of his turban, and displayed his hair to the crowd which surrounded him. It was plaited and matted into two thin coils upon the top of his head, and its length had not been by any means exaggerated by Punchirala. The sanyasi spoke only a strange language, unintelligible to the Tamils and Sinhalese in the crowd, but there stood by him an old Tamil man who interpreted what he said.

Babun led Silindu up to the sanyasi and dropped the money in the bowl. He explained what he wanted to the old Tamil, who understood and spoke (very badly) Sinhalese. The crowd pressed forward to listen. The sanyasi and his interpreter muttered together. The old man then addressed the crowd, and told them that the holy man could not consult the god, or give an answer, with them pressing upon him. There was much talking and excitement, but at last a large circle was cleared, and the crowd was induced to move away out of earshot. Most of the people squatted down, and, though they could not hear a word of what followed, they watched in hope of some exciting development.

Babun and Silindu squatted down in front of the sanyasi. Karlinahami, Hinnihami, and the others of their party stood behind them. Silindu, weak and dejected though he was, for the first time for several days seemed to take some interest in what was passing. It had been arranged that Babun should explain the case to the sanyasi.

'Will you tell the holy man,' he said to the interpreter, 'that we are poor folk and ask pardon of him? This man is my wife's father, a hunter, a very poor man. There is also a yakka who lives in the banian-trees in the jungle over there' (Babun made a sweep with his arm towards the west). 'This yakka has entered this man, and his life is going from him. Why has the yakka entered the man? There is another man in the village; that man is skilled in charms and magic, and is angry with this man. Therefore, he charmed the devil to do this. Well, then, when this had happened, the woman went to him and prayed him to charm the devil away again. Then he said, "Take your brother to

Beragama, and pray to the god there at the great festival." So we walked and walked to this place with the sick man, and we went in the perahera and called to the god. But the god does not hear us, and the man's life is going from him. Then the woman went again to the man, for he too is here, and told him. He said, "I can do nothing; take the man to the holy man who sits under the banian-tree, and make inquiry of him." So we waited for the lucky hour, and have brought him.'

The interpreter talked in the strange tongue with the sanyasi, and then said to Babun:

'The holy man says that the offering is too small.'

'Father, it is all we have. We are very poor. Rain never falls upon our fields, and we have no land. We pray him to help us.'

There was another muttered conversation, and then the interpreter said:

'It is very little for so great a thing. But the holy man will help you.'

The little group became very still; every one watched the sanyasi anxiously. He muttered to himself, fixed his eyes on the ground in front of him, made marks in the sand with his finger, and swayed his body from side to side. Then looking at Silindu intently he began to speak very volubly. Silindu watched him, fascinated. At last the sanyasi stopped, and the interpreter addressed them:

'The holy man says thus: it is true that a devil of the jungle has entered the man. This devil is of great power. Why has this happened? The man is a foolish man. There has come into the holy man's mind another man, his face marked with scars, and one-eyed. He is a vederala, very skilled in charms. You have not told why the one-eyed man is angry, but the holy man knows because of his holiness and wisdom. The one-eyed man came and said, "Give me your daughter," but this man, being mad, refused and spoke evil. Then the one-eyed man was very angry, and went away and made a charm over the devil, and the devil entered the man. When the one-eyed man made the charm he said to the devil: "Unless she be given to me, do not leave him."'

A cry broke from Hinnihami; she covered her face with her

hands, and crouched in fear upon the ground. The interpreter paid no attention to her.

'Now even the one-eyed man cannot loose the charm, so he has sent you to the god. The god is of great power over devils: he heard your prayer, and he said to this devil, "Leave the man." But the yakka answered, fighting against the power, "Something must be given." The master said, "Unless she be given, do not leave the man. Am I to die for this foolish man's sake?" Then the god said, "Yes something must be given – either the man or the girl." The holy man knows this, and says that you must remain here, and take the man every night in the perahera until the night of the full moon, and on the morning of the next day you must return to the village. But on the evening of the first day's journey, the one-eyed man will meet you in an open stony place beside two palu-trees. Then you must go to him and say, "There is the girl; take her." He will take the girl, and the devil will leave the man. Otherwise, if you do not do this the man will die, for something must be given – either the man or the girl. Remember, too, that the girl cannot be given during the festival."

Hinnihami pressed her body against the ground, but her eyes were dry now. She was broken: tired and numb with fear and despair; she had always known that it was she who was bringing death upon her father. Instinctively, like a wild animal against a trap, she had fought against the idea of giving herself to Punchirala. At the thought of her body touching his, the skin seemed to shrink against her bones. Silindu was everything to her, and she knew now she was everything to him. At first she had felt that she was being driven inevitably to sacrifice herself; but when Karlinahami returned from Punchirala's compound, and told them of the pilgrimage, hope came to her. The hardships and excitement of the road, her ecstasy before the god, had driven away her first feeling of despair. The god would certainly help them. But fear had crept in again at the first sight of Punchirala, and as she listened to his talk with Karlinahami her hope grew cold. Now she knew that she must inevitably sacrifice herself. Had not the sanyasi known the truth which

Babun had not disclosed? She knew that not even the god could help her; she had heard his words, 'Yes, something must be given – either the man or the girl.' Once more evil had come out of the jungle.

The effect upon the other listeners had also been great. The holy man had seen what Babun had hidden; they knew well that they had heard from him the reply of the god. They walked back to the temple talking about it in low voices. There was no suggestion of doubt in any one as to what should be done. Even Silindu had given in. The god had spoken; it was fate, the inevitable. The girl would be given.

The remainder of the festival passed slowly for them. They followed the perahera dispirited, and called upon the god nightly. But there was no hope or even doubt now to excite them. Silindu, listless, waited for his release; Hinnihami was cowed and dulled by despair. The nights passed, and the morning following the new moon came; and they went down dutifully to the river to take part in the cutting of the waters. They were a melancholy little group among the laughing, joking crowd, which stood knee-deep in the river. And when the supreme moment came, and the kapurala cut the waters, and the crowd with a shout splashed high over themselves and one another the waters which would bring them good fortune through the coming year, Hinnihami stood among them weeping.

The pilgrimage was over, and a line of returning pilgrims began at once to stream across the river westwards. The old man and the fisher and his wife said good-bye to them, for they felt that it was not right for them, being strangers, to be present at what was to take place upon the homeward journey. Then they too set out. They walked all that day slowly – for Silindu was very weak – and in silence. When the shadows began to lengthen the jungle became thinner, and the ground more stony. They knew that they must be nearing the place. The track turned and twisted through the scrub; the air was very still. They passed a bend, and there before them stood the vederala under some palu-trees. They stopped for a moment and looked at one another. Karlinahami touched Silindu on the arm. He took Hinnihami by the hand and went up to Punchirala. His eyes seemed to be fixed upon something far away beyond Punchirala; he spoke very slowly:

'Here is the girl; take her.'

Punchirala looked at Hinnihami and smiled.

'It is well,' he said.

Silindu turned, and with Karlinahami and Babun walked on down the track. Neither of them looked back. Hinnihami was left standing by the vederala, her arms hanging limply by her side, her eyes looking on the ground.

CHAPTER VI

IT became clear on the morning after Hinnihami had been given to the vederala that the sanyasi had rightly interpreted the will of the god, and that the devil had left Silindu. His eyes no longer presented the glazed appearance, which is the sign of possession. He ate eagerly of the scanty morning meal; and, though still weak, walked with a vigour unknown to him since the night when he fell beneath the banian-trees in the jungle. Throughout the homeward journey strength and health continued to return to him; and by the time they reached the village, the colour of his skin showed that he had been restored to his normal condition.

Though they travelled very slowly, they had not again seen the vederala and Hinnihami on the way home. Punchirala made no haste to return to the village, and he only appeared there two days after Silindu arrived. He showed no signs of pleasure in his triumph; he was more quiet and thoughtful than usual. In the house he seemed to his mother to be uneasy, and a little afraid of Hinnihami.

The girl had yielded herself to him in silence. In the long journey together through the jungle he had, without success, tried many methods of breaking or bending her spirit. But he had failed: his jeers and his irony, his anger and his embraces, had all been received by her in sullen silence. He would have put her down to be merely a passionless, stupid village woman had he not seen the light and anger in her eyes, and the shudder that passed over her body when he touched her.

On the morning after she arrived in the village, Hinnihami was alone in Punchirala's compound; the vederala had gone out, and his mother was in the house. She saw Silindu coming along the path, and ran out eagerly to meet him. They sat down under a tamarind tree, just outside the stile in the compound fence.

'The yakka has gone,' said Silindu. 'The god drove him out

after the vederala took you. But now what to do? The house is empty without you, child.'

'I must come back, Appochchi. I cannot live in this house.'

'But, is it safe? Will not he bring evil again upon us? The god said one must be given, and now if I take you again, will he not kill you?'

'The god said that one must be given, and it was done. I was given, and the man took me. Surely the gods cannot lie. The evil has been driven out; and as for the man, I am not frightened of him.'

'Ané!' said the mocking voice of the vederala behind them. 'They are not frightened of the man. Oh no, nor of the devils either, I suppose.'

Silindu and Hinnihami got up; the old fear came upon Silindu when he saw Punchirala, but the girl turned angrily upon the vederala, who was astonished by her violence.

'Punchirala,'[1] she said, 'I am not frightened of you. The god did not say I was to live with you. There is no giving of food or clothing. I was given that the devil might leave my father. Was the god disobeyed? I was given to you, you dog; the devil has flown; the god heard us there at Beragama; he will not allow you again to do evil.'

'Mother, mother, come out! Listen to the woman I brought to the house; she has become a vederala. The pilgrimage has made her a sanyasi, I think, knowing the god's mind, skilled in magic.'

'Keep your words for the women of the house. I am going.'

'And are there no other charms, Silindu? No other devils in the trees? You have learned wisdom surely from a wise woman.'

'Do not listen to him, Appochchi. He can no longer harm us. The god has aided us.' She turned upon Punchirala. 'Do you wish me to stay in the house? Yes, there are still devils in the trees. Do not I too come from the jungle? I shall be like a yakkini to you in the house, you dog. You can tell them, they say, by the eyes which do not blink. Rightly the village women call me

[1] Hinnihami addresses Punchirala by name, and thereby shows him that she does not regard herself as living with him as his wife.

yakkini. I will stay with you. Look at my arms. Are they not as strong as a man's arms? I will stay with you, but as you lie by my side in the house I will strangle you, Punchirala.'

Punchirala instinctively stepped back, and Hinnihami laughed.

'Ohé! Are you frightened, Punchirala? The binder of yakkas is frightened of the yakkini. You can tell her, they say, because her eyes are red and unblinking, and because she neither fears nor loves. It is better for you that I should go – to the trees from which I came, mighty vederala. Otherwise, I would strangle you, and eat you in the house. Come, Appochchi, we will go out into the jungle together again as we did long ago – aiyo! the long time. I was a little thing then – and the little sister too. Come, Appochchi; do not fear this Rodiya dog: he is frightened: and now I will never leave you.'

Punchirala was really frightened. He stood and watched the girl walk slowly away with Silindu along the path. Things had not happened quite as he had expected or hoped. He had enjoyed his first triumph over the girl, but he had soon grown to doubt whether her continued presence in his house would add to his comfort. He had felt, without understanding, that the giving of her body to him had only made her spirit more unyielding. Even on the way from Beragama he had felt nervous and uncomfortable with her. He was angered by his defeat and by her taunts, but he watched her disappear with a distinct feeling of relief.

The vederala made no further attempt to molest Silindu, and the next nine months were a period of unwonted prosperity and happiness in the 'Vedda' family. Towards the end of October great clouds rolled up from the north-east, and great rains broke over the jungle. For days the rain fell steadily, ceaselessly. The tank filled and ran over; the dry sandy channels became torrents, sweeping down old rotten trunks and great trees through the jungle; a mist of moisture rose from the parched earth, and hung grey upon the face of the jungle. Suddenly the ground became green, and soon the grass stood waist-high beneath the under-growth. The earth at last was sodden; and as the rain still fell and the streams overflowed, the water spread out in a vast sheet beneath the trees.

Not for forty years, it was said, had rain fallen so abundantly. A great chena crop was assured. The more energetic began to talk of rice cultivation, now that the tank was full, and to regret the want of seed paddy. Then a rumour spread that the Government was going to make advances of seed, and at last one day the Korala Mahatmaya appeared in the village, and the rumour was confirmed. Promissory-notes were signed; buffaloes were borrowed to turn up the soil of the fields; and at last, after twelve years, the village again saw paddy standing green in the water below their tank.

Silindu's family, principally owing to Babun, had a large share in the prosperity which came to the village from the wonderful chena and rice-crops. Their store was full of kurakkan and millet and rice. They were well fed, and even Silindu became happy. After the return of Hinnihami he seemed to change greatly. They were almost always together, and the fearlessness which she had shown towards Punchirala, and which seemed to have changed her suddenly from a child into a woman, inspired him. The fear of evil overhanging him no longer oppressed him. He worked with Babun cheerfully in the chena and rice-fields: he began again to talk with Punchi Menika. And sometimes he would sit in the compound and tell his strange stories to her and to the child, who had been born to her eighteen months before, and he was happy as he had been happy with her and with Hinnihami years ago when they were children. His happiness and Hinnihami's was greatly increased when she gave birth to a daughter. The child, conceived during the pilgrimage, was a pledge to them from the god that, as his word had been obeyed, the evil had been finally conquered. To the physical joy which Hinnihami felt as she suckled the child, was added her exultation in the knowledge that she was holding in her arms a charm against the evil which had threatened Silindu. Her hatred for the father only increased therefore her love for his child.

But the love and care which she showed from the moment of her birth to Punchi Nona, as she called her daughter, were from the first to be shared with another. On the morning following the evening on which the child was born, Silindu came back from the jungle carrying in his arms a fawn newly dropped by its mother. He went straight to Hinnihami, who lay in the hut nursing the child, and kneeling down by her placed the fawn in her arms. Hinnihami with a little laugh took it, and nestling it against the child was soon suckling the one at one breast and the other at the other. Silindu watched in silence: he was very serious.

'It is well, it is well,' he said when he saw that the fawn was sucking quietly and nestling against Hinnihami and the child.

'The little weakling,' said Hinnihami, gently touching with her fingers the soft skin of the fawn. 'How hungry for milk the little one is! Where has it come from?'

'It has come to you from the jungle. The gods have sent it.'

She bent her head, and very softly drew her lips backwards and forwards over its back.

'It takes the milk like the child. Has the god given another gift, Appochchi?'

'The god sent it. Last night I went to the water-hole, but nothing came while the moon was up. Then clouds gathered and the moon was hidden, and it became very dark. I heard a doe cry near by in pain, "Amma, amma,"[1] but it was too dark to see, so I lay down and slept on the top of the high rock. I woke up with the first light, and as I lay there, I heard below the moving of something among the leaves. Very slowly I looked over the rock, and there below in the undergrowth I saw the back of a doe. Her head was down, hidden by the leaves, and she murmured, licking something on the grass. Slowly, slowly I took up my gun and leaned it over the rock and fired. Everything was hidden from me by the smoke, and I lay quiet until the wind blew it from before me. When I looked again I saw the doe stand there still, the blood running down her side; and she stretched up her head toward me from the jungle, and her great eyes rolled back with fear and showed white, and she opened her mouth and cried

---

[1] Mother.

terribly to me. I was sorry for her pain, and I said, "Hush, mother, the evil has come. What use to cry? Lie down that death may come to you easily." But again she stretched out her neck toward me, and cried loud in pain, "Amma! amma! Aiyo! aiyo! It is you who have brought the evil, Yakka. To the child here that I dropped last night and that lies now between my feet. Little son, I have borne you to be food for the jackal and the leopard." Then I came down from the rock and stood by her and said, "Mother, the daughter at home this night bore a child. I will take this one too to her, and she will give it the breast." Then she stretched out her head, and she cried out again, and fell dead upon the ground by the side of the fawn.'

Hinnihami pressed the fawn to her.

'Yes, he has come to me out of the jungle, a sign from the god, a great charm against evil. Did not the god himself take the doe as his mistress? They told it to us at Beragama. And now in the same night he has sent me a son and a daughter from the jungle.'

So Hinnihami suckled the child and the fawn together. The village looked on with astonishment and disapproval. 'The woman is as mad as the father,' was the general comment. It was commonly rumoured that she showed more love for Punchi Appu, as the fawn was called, than for her daughter. And though she did not realise it herself, it was true. 'The son from the jungle' inspired in her a passionate love and tenderness – the great eyes which watched her and the wonderful skin that she was never tired of caressing. He had come to her out of the jungle, with something of the mystery and exaltation which she had felt in Beragama towards the god who went by upon the elephant. And her love was increased by the attachment of Punchi Appu to her. Long before Punchi Nona could crawl about the compound, the fawn would trot along by her side crying to be taken up and fed; and even after it grew old enough to feed upon grass and leaves, it never left her, following her always about the house and compound, and through the village and jungle.

The year of the great rains and rice and plenty was followed by a year of scarcity and sickness. For four months, from June to October, the sun beat down from a cloudless sky. The great wind from the south-west failed at last, but even then the rain did not come, and the withering heat lay still and heavy over the jungle. The little puddle thick with mud in the tank, which supplied the village with water, dried up, and the women had to go daily four miles to fetch water from an abandoned tank in the jungle. In November the chenas were still standing black and unsown. At last a little rain fell and the seed was sown. The crop just showed green above the ground, and drought came again, and the young shoots died down.

Then, when it was too late to save the crops, the rains came, and with them sickness. Want had already begun to be felt by bodies weakened by the long drought, and fever and dysentery swept over the country. There was not a family in Beddagama which did not suffer, nor a house in which death did not take the old or the children. The doctor Mahatmaya, whom Punchirala despised, appeared in the village, bringing the medicines which he despised still more; but his efforts were no more or less successful than those of the village vederala. When at last the sickness passed away, it was found that the village had lost sixteen out of its forty-one inhabitants. And the jungle pressed in and claimed two of the eight houses, after dysentery and fever had taken the men, the women, and their children, who lived there.

Even Silindu's house did not escape: there death took its toll of the young. First Punchi Menika's child sickened and then Punchi Nona. Day after day the mothers, helpless, watched the fever come and shake the children's bodies, and sap and waste their strength. The wail of the two women, each for her dead child, was raised in one night.

It was Silindu who seemed to feel the loss of the children more than any one else in the house. This time clearly the envious powers had grudged him his little happiness. He had been foolish to show his pleasure in the children crawling about the house. He had brought disaster upon them and upon himself.

The misery he had felt at losing Punchi Menika came upon him again. It was his own fault: he was a fool to tempt the evil powers that stood around him eager for their opportunity.

After the first wild outburst of grief, Punchi Menika and Hinnihami felt their loss less than Silindu. The death of the child is what every mother must continually expect. They had seen it too long in the village to be surprised at their own suffering: the birth of children every year and then the coming of the fever to carry them off. Their grief was lightened by the feeling of resignation to the inevitable. And in Hinnihami's case there was a further consolation. She still had Punchi Appu, in whose attachment she could forget the child's death. All her love for the child was now merged in her love for him: he was the mysterious gift and pledge of the god; and she felt that so long as he followed by her side, so long as she felt the caress of his lips upon her hand, no real evil could come to her.

Hinnihami's extraordinary love for the deer was well known in the village, and had never been approved. At first it was regarded merely as the folly of the 'mad' woman. These views were, however, very rarely expressed to the girl herself, for most of the villagers stood in some fear of her passionate anger. But about the time when the epidemic of fever and dysentery was decreasing, a new feeling towards them made its appearance in the village. It was started by Punchirala. 'The mad woman and her child,' he would say. 'What sort of madness is that? An evil woman, an evil woman. I have some knowledge of charms and magic. I took her to my house to live with me. But did I keep her? I drove her away very soon. I did not want the evil eye and a worker of evil to bring misfortune on my house. My mother knows, for she heard her call herself a yakkini. Only because of my knowledge of charms was I able to keep away the evil with which she threatened me. And then comes this deer which they say is found in the jungle. Was not the woman herself in travail that very night? Do not she-devils give birth to devils? Do village women suckle deer? Surely it is a devil, born of a devil. Look at the evil that fell upon the village when it came. The crops withered, and the old and the young died. It has brought us want and disease and death.'

The village soon became to believe in Punchirala's opinions. Small children were hurried away out of sight of Hinnihami as she passed. The deer was certainly a devil, who had brought misfortune on the village. Some said that at night it went out and ate the corpses in the new graves. It had been clear for some time that the ill-feeling against them had been growing, when an event occurred which required immediate action. The son of the headman died suddenly, and apparently for no cause. Then it was remembered that, three days before, the child had been carrying some leaves when he met the deer and Hinnihami. The deer had gone up to the child and tried to nibble the leaves, but the boy had snatched them away. The headman and the vederala were convinced that Hinnihami and the deer were the direct cause of the child's death. There was much talk between Babehami and Punchirala; other villagers were sent for; there was much coming and going and discussion in the headman's compound, and eventually action was decided upon.

The next day Hinnihami was collecting firewood in an old chena. The deer was with her, feeding at a little distance from her upon the young leaves and grass. Suddenly she was aroused by noise and movements near her. A small band of men and boys from the village had crept quietly through the jungle, and now were between her and the deer. As she looked up the first stone was thrown: it missed its mark, but another followed, and struck with a thud upon the deer's side. He bounded forward. Hinnihami cried out and ran towards him: at the sound of her voice he stopped and looked round. A shower of stones fell about him: thin stream of blood began to trickle down his flanks; suddenly he plunged forward upon his head, his two forelegs broken at the knees. A cheer broke from the men. Hinnihami, as she dashed forward, was caught by two men and flung backwards upon the ground. She fell heavily and for a moment was stunned; then she heard the long, bleating cry of pain, and saw the deer vainly trying to raise itself upon its broken legs among the jeering knot of men. She felt the blood surge up to her forehead and temples as a wave of anger came over her, and she flung herself upon the two men who barred her path. Swinging their arms wildly, they gave her blow upon blow with the open hand upon her head and breast. Her jacket was torn into shreds, and at last she fell exhausted.

The sight of the bleeding deer and the woman lying on the ground, naked to the waist, seemed to send a wave of lust and cruelty through the men. They tore Hinnihami's cloth from her, and, taking her by her arms, dragged her naked up to the deer.

'Bring the vesi to her child,' they shouted. 'Comfort your yakka, yakkini. Is there no milk in your breasts for him now?'

They held her that she might see what they did. The deer was moaning in pain. One of the men cut a thick stick and struck him upon the hind legs until they were broken. Hinnihami fought and struggled, but she was powerless in their hands. At length, when they had become tired of torturing them, they threw her down by the deer's side and went away.

Hinnihami was unhurt, but she was stunned by the violence of anger and horror. The deer moaned from time to time. She tried to lift him with some vague idea of carrying him back to the house. But he screamed with pain at the slightest movement, and he had grown too big for her to carry. She felt that he was dying. She flung herself down by him, caressing his head, and calling to him not to leave her. 'Punchi Appu! Punchi Appu!' she kept repeating, 'you must not die. Surely the god who gave you to me will save you. Punchi Appu, Punchi Appu, you cannot die.'

Then gradually a sense only of dull despair settled upon her. She sat through the long day unconscious of the passing of time. She was unaware when the deer died; she knew that he was dead now, and that with him everything had died for her. There was nothing for her to live for now, and already she felt life slipping from her. She thought of the child who had died too: she had missed her, and grieved for her, but she had never loved the child as she loved the deer. He had come to her, a wild thing from the jungle, the god's mysterious gift. Now he was lying there dead, his broken limbs twisted under him, the dead white eyes bulging, the tongue hanging out from the open mouth. She shuddered as she remembered the scene, shuddered as she recalled the thud of the stones and the blows.

She was found by Silindu next morning, still sitting naked by the body of the deer, her hair wet with the dew, and her limbs stiff with the chill of the jungle at night. He tried in vain to rouse her. She recognised him. 'Let me be, Appochchi,' she kept repeating. 'Let me die here, for he is dead. Let me die here, Appochchi.'

Then Silindu wrapped her cloth about her, and carried her in his arms to the house. She cried a little when she felt his tears fall upon her, but after that she showed no more signs of grief. She lay in the house, silent, and resigned to die. She had even ceased to think or feel now. Life had no more a hold upon her, and in the hour before dawn in deep sleep she allowed it to slip gently from her.

CHAPTER VII

SILINDU knew well now that Hinnihami had been a victim to save him. Both the devil and the god had said, 'Either the man or the girl must be given.' It was the girl who had been given; but it was he who should have died, when the devil still possessed him. He knew now, when it was too late, that in giving Hinnihami to the vederala he was giving her to certain death. He had gained nothing by his first refusal of the vederala but pain and trouble, and now the bitterest of griefs. In the end he had lost her utterly; now indeed the house was empty. He was a fool, yes, a fool; he knew that; but how can a man know how to walk surrounded by all the snares of evil and disaster? A man may wash himself clean of oil, but however much he rubs himself he will never rub off fate. And then there was Punchirala; it was he who was the real cause of the evil. Why had he ever come with his hateful face into the compound? He would go in the early morning and take his gun and shoot the vederala dead as he came out of his house. And yet what would be the good of that now – now that Hinnihami was dead? It would only be more evil. It would be useless. It was useless for him to do anything now.

For days Silindu sat about the compound 'thinking and thinking' as Punchi Menika called it. She alone had any influence with him, and even she had no power to console him. In time grief lost its first bitterness, and he sank into a perpetual state of sullen despair. An air of gloom and disaster seemed to hang about the compound.

It was not long after the life of the village had been stirred by the death of Hinnihami that another event happened which caused no little excitement. It was seen that Babehami, the headman, was having a house built on the open ground adjoining his compound; and as soon as it was finished there came to live in it a man from Kamburupitiya, known as Fernando. Many of the villagers had had dealings with him: he kept a small boutique in Kamburupitiya, and lent money on the usual, and even more than the usual, interest. He was not a Sinhalese, and spoke Sinhalese very badly. Some people said he was a Tamil: his black skin and curly black hair pointed to the fact that he had Kaffir blood in his veins.

He was a typical town man, cunning, unscrupulous, with a smattering of education. He wore the ordinary native cloth, but above it a shirt and coat, and the villagers therefore called him Mahatmaya. It was obvious that some very peculiar circumstances had brought such a man to settle down in a village like Beddagama. The fact was that the headman and many of the villagers were deeply in his debt. The failure of the previous year's chena crop had made it impossible to recover anything; in fact he was pestered with requests for further loans to tide the debtors over the hot season, until the chenas could again be sown.

The creditor was faced with an unpleasant alternative. If he refused further loans he would lose what he had lent already through the death or emigration of his debtors, or they would borrow from others, and thus make it difficult for him to recover. On the other hand the complete failure of the chena crop made his own position far from easy: the debt outstanding together with the interest would be in itself a heavy charge on the next crop, even if it were a really good one. To be safe in giving still more credit, he required additional security.

It was Babehami, the headman, who devised a scheme to meet these difficulties. Four acres of chena would be allowed to each debtor: the permits would be given in favour of the debtors, who were to assign their rights to Fernando for one-fifth of the crop. It was tacitly understood that if the four-fifths of the crop exceeded the amount of the loans and interest, the debts would be considered cancelled. Fernando was to come to the village, and himself supervise the working of the chenas. Practically, therefore, the money-lender was hiring labour for the cultivation of chenas for one-fifth of the crop, an exceedingly paying transaction; while his rights and power of action for the outstanding debts remained unaffected. The villagers were completely in his hands, and both sides were fully aware of it. The whole transaction, certainly, so far as the headman was concerned, was illegal. Babehami knew this; but his needs were pressing, and his own profit would be great; for, while his consent was purchased by the cancellation of his debts, by a private arrangement with Fernando, his own four acres of chena were not assigned to the money-lender.

To the villagers Fernando was, owing to his dress and habits, a Mahatmaya. He did not treat them as his equals, and they — being in his debt — treated him as a superior. He was, however, on terms of intimacy with Babehami; and although he had a small boy with him as servant, he took all his meals in the headman's house.

Punchi Menika very soon attracted Fernando's attention. Her face and form would have been remarkable even in a town: to find her among the squalid women of so squalid a village astonished him. He wanted a woman to live with him; he was always wanting a woman; and it would be far more comfortable to have his food cooked for him than to go always to the headman for his meals. He anticipated no difficulty; she was a mere village woman, and the husband was a village boor, and in his debt.

Despite his confidence Fernando decided to act cautiously. He knew very little about villages, but he knew the many proverbs about women and trouble; and he had heard many tales of violence and murder, of which women had been the cause. He was quite alone among people whom he did not really understand, far away from the boutiques and police court, the busy little town which he understood, and where alone he really felt secure. He was a timid man, and he hated the jungle; and, though he despised these people who lived in it, he was not comfortable with them.

His first move was to try to learn something about the family from the headman. He sounded Babehami cautiously. The result pleased him greatly. They were bad people according to the headman — veddas, gipsies, traffickers in evil, whores, and vagabonds. By evil charms they had enticed Babun to their compound, and now they boasted that he, the brother of the headman's wife, had married Punchi Menika. They were dangerous people; they had brought misfortune and death into the village. Fernando was not greatly impressed by their reputation for working harm 'by magic'; as became a townman, he was somewhat sceptical; but what was clear to him was that the headman hated the whole family; they would get in no eventuality any help or sympathy from him. This knowledge was as valuable as it was pleasing to him.

Then one evening he surprised them by coming and chatting to Babun almost as if he were an equal. It was evening, just about the time before the lamps are lit in the house, when the air grows cool, and the wind dies down, and the afterglow of the setting sun is in the sky. The work in the chena for the man, and in the house for the woman, was over. Babun was squatting in the compound near the house, and Punchi Menika stood behind him, leaning against the doorpost. From time to time a word or two was spoken but for the most part they were content to allow the silence of the evening to descend upon them, as they watched with vacant eyes the light fade out of the sky.

Punchi Menika brought the wooden mortar in which the grain was pounded, turned it upside down, and dusted the top with a piece of cloth.

'Will you sit down, aiya?' said Babun. Fernando sat down upon it. Babun squatted opposite to him, while Punchi Menika stood behind, leaning against the doorpost.

'Well, Babun,' said Fernando, 'will the chena crop be good, do you think?'

'Who can say, aiya, who can say? Only a fool measures his grain before it is on the threshing-floor.'

'Then all these villagers do that, for they are all fools. Aiyo! what cattle! what trouble they give a man!'

'We are poor men, aiya, and ignorant.'

'I'm not thinking of you, Babun, but of the others. There is only one man in the village; all say that, and I've seen it myself. But the others! They will ruin me. How much do they owe me! Only a very good crop will pay it, but they don't care. They don't fence the chena or watch it; they sit and sleep in the compound, and the deer and pig go off with my rupees in their bellies. Isn't that true?'

'It's true, aiya.'

'And what can I do, a town man, with all these chenas? I ought to have a gambaraya.'[1]

'Yes, you want a gambaraya.'

'So I thought, and I thought too, "This Babun is the only man in the village, why shouldn't he be my gambaraya?" Well, what do you say? You could look after the other chenas, and also cultivate your own?'

Babun was silent with astonishment; it was a piece of good fortune which he could never have dreamed of.

'I would give you one-twentieth of the crop, after the fifth had been paid to the cultivators,' Fernando went on. 'Would you do it for that?'

'Yes, aiya, I will do it for that, gladly.'

'Very well, that's settled. You are my gambaraya now.'

Fernando sighed and stretched himself. 'What a place this jungle is!' he said. 'It is not fit for a sensible man to live in. Of course these other villagers, if they went anywhere else, what could they do, the cattle? They do not know the east from the west, as the tale says. If they get into a bazaar they are frightened, and run about like a scared bull. But you, Babun, you are young and strong; you are a knowing man. Why do you starve here when you could eat rice and grow fat elsewhere?'

'So my sister and her man said, aiya! They wanted me to go away and marry in another village — over there; rain falls and rice grows there. But it is a great evil to live in a strange place and among strangers.'

Fernando laughed. 'An evil you call it! But how many have got wealth and fortune by going to strange places! Have you not heard of Maha Potana? Many years ago it was all trees and jungle like this, and no one lived there. Then they built the great

---

[1] A gambaraya is technically a man who oversees the cultivation of rice-fields for the owners, and is paid usually by a share of the crop.

tank in the jungle, and people went there from all the villages of
the west – poor men living in villages like this. Now it is a town,
and all are rich there, and eating rice.'

'Yes, aiya, we know that. The tank was built in my father's
time. And the Korala Mahatmaya and the Ratemahatmaya came
to the village and spoke as you speak now. And they said that
land would be given to all that went there, and water from the
tank for the cultivation of rice. It was in a year, I remember my
father telling me, when rain had not fallen – like the last crop
with us – and there was want in the village, and many died of
fever. They urged my father to go, for he was a good man: they
knew that. And my father said to them – so he told me – "How
can I go to this strange place? Can I take the woman and the
child with me? I have no house there, and no money to buy in the
bazaar. Among strangers and in strange places evil comes. Here
my father lived, and his father before him, in this house; and
they cleared the chenas as I do, and from time to time when rain
fell sowed rice below the tank. What folly for me to leave my
home and field and the chena to meet evil in strange places." My
father said this to the headman, and all the other men of the
village also refused to go, except one man – Appu they called
him; he went with his wife, and was given land under Maha
Potana. And nothing was heard of Appu for many months; and
his brother, who still lived here, at last went to Maha Potana to
inquire about him. And when he came there the people told him
that Appu was dead of the fever, and that his wife had gone
away, and no one knew where she had gone.'

'But people died of fever in Beddagama.'

'Yes, aiya, of course many people die of fever here too. But
they die among their relations, and friends, and people who are
known to them; in houses where their fathers lived before them.
Surely it is a more bitter thing to die in a strange place. I am a
poor man and ignorant, and I cannot explain it to you better.
There is always trouble and evil in strange places; when a man
goes even upon a journey or pilgrimage to Kamburupitiya or
Maha Potana or Beragama, always, aiya, he is troubled and
afraid – in the bazaars and boutiques and on the roads people

unknown to him — and everywhere he is thinking of his village, and his house, and the tank, and the jungle paths which he knows there, and people living in the village, all of whom he knows. That is why a man will not leave his village, even when the crops fail and there is no food; no, not even when the headmen come — and they come now every year — and say, "There is good land to be given in such a place, there is work upon such a road, or in such a village, why starve here?" I have heard people say that far away in the west there are large towns, Colombo and Kalutara and Galle, where every one has food and money always; but, aiya, not even to those towns do you see a man going who has been born and lived all his life in a village."

'Am I not now among strangers? What evil will befall me?'

'May the gods keep it away from you, aiya. But how can a man tell what evil is before him? But you are not an ignorant village man like us, and besides after the chena is reaped you will return to your house.'

Fernando was silent for a while. When he spoke again he had a curiously seductive effect upon his listeners. His low, soft voice and broken Sinhalese, the languorousness and softness which seemed to pervade him fascinated them even more than what he said.

'What can the buffalo born in the fold know of the jungle? or does the wild buffalo know how to work in the rice-fields? I was born far away across the sea on the coast. I was only a little child when they brought me to Colombo to live there in the shop which my father kept. He had no fear to leave his village and to cross the sea, nor had he any desire to go back again there. He was a rich man. Ohé! what a town is Colombo. There we lived in a great building, and all around us were houses and houses, and people and people: no jungle or snakes or wild beasts; not even a paddy-field or a cocoanut-tree. Always streets and people walking, walking backwards and forwards on the red roads (and very few even known to you by sight), and bullock-carts and carriages and rickshaws, hundreds upon hundreds. And there are houses, very high, as high as the hill at Beragama, full of white Mahatmayas and their women, always coming and going from the ships. How many times have I stood outside when a boy and watched them, always laughing and talking loud, like madmen, and dancing, men and women together. And how fair are the women, fair as the lotus-flower as the tale says; very fair and very shameless.'

'Is it true then that the women of the white Mahatmayas are shameless?' broke in Punchi Menika.

'In Colombo all say they are shameless. Very fair, very mad, and very shameless. Their eyes are like cat's eyes. The proverb says, "If the eyes of a woman are like the eyes of a cat, evil comes to the man who looks into them." The hair of the English Mahatmayas' women is very fair, the colour of the young cocoanut-flowers. Yes, they are mad. In the evening strange music is played by many men sitting high up near the roof; then every Mahatmaya takes a woman in his arms, and looking into her eyes goes round and round very quickly on the floor.'

'Aiya, aiya, is this a true tale?'

'Why should I tell you what is false? Did I not live twenty years there in Colombo? It is a great town. In the morning I went and walked on the stone road that has been built into the sea, and within is the harbour, full always of great ships bigger than villages. Always the Mahatmayas are coming and going in the great ships; from where they come and where they go no one can tell. You stand upon the stone road, and you see the great ship come in across the sea in the morning, filled with white Mahatmayas, and in the evening it carries them out again across the sea. They are all very rich, and for a thing that costs one shilling they willingly give five. Also they are never quiet, going here and there very quickly, and doing nothing. Very many are afraid of them, for suddenly they grow very angry, their faces become red, and they strike any one who is near with the closed hand.'

Fernando stopped. He had become quite excited as he recalled his life in Colombo in his youth. He had forgotten where he was. Suddenly he became aware of his surroundings, the little village so far away from everything; the ignorant, uncouth villager who listened to him; the woman behind him for whose sake he had come to the hut, and whom for the moment he had forgotten. For a while Babun did not like to disturb his silence, then he asked diffidently:

'But aiya, if Colombo is your village, how is it that you now live in Kamburupitiya?'

Fernando laughed. 'What talk is this of villages?' he said. Everywhere here the question is, "Of what village is he?" And then, "He is of Beddagama or Bogama, or Beragama, or any gama."[1] And the liver in villages says, as you did but now, "How can I leave my gama?" Did I not tell you that I am of no village? My father's village is beyond the sea, and they say that the father's village is the son's. I have never seen that village; I have forgotten its name. I was born in Colombo, which is no village, but a town. Aiyo! what a town it is! How pleasant! The houses and the noise and smell of the bazaar for miles, and the dust and people everywhere! What folly to live here, like a sanyasi on the top of a bare rock! Perhaps one day I shall return to Colombo, and live in a great house, as my father did. My father was a rich man, but always gambling; no money stayed in the house. And I spent much money upon women. There was a nautch-girl from the coast; her eyes had made me mad, and she devoured me. It was always rupees, and bracelets, and anklets, and silk cloths. Then my father was very angry, for all the money had gone on the gambling and jewellery. There was no money to pay the merchants for goods for the shop, but worst of all he had no money for gambling. The girl had taunted me because I had come empty handed, saying that she would shame me openly if I came back again with nothing. So I again asked my father for money. He drove me away, cursing me; so I went into the shop, and took goods and sold them, and taking two handfuls of silver flung them down before the girl. But when my father found what I had done, he cursed me again, and beat me, and drove me out of the house, saying, that if I returned he would give me to the police. I ran out very sad because of the girl. I was also sorry that I had given her both handfuls of silver, and had not kept one for

---

[1] Gama means a village.

myself. I stood at a street corner thinking that now I would die of hunger, and that it would be better to hang myself. Just then there passed a Moorman, Cassim, a man of Kalutara, a merchant, whom I had often seen in my father's shop. He laughed at me when he saw me, and said, speaking Tamil, "Now I see that the feet of the girl have danced away with the old man's wealth and the young man's life.". At that the tears ran down my face, and I told him all that had happened. Then he said, "Come with me to Kalutara. You can sell there for me in my shop." So I went with him to Kalutara, and stayed there selling for him for two years. After that he sent me to sell for him in Kamburupitiya, and there I now live, and have a shop of my own.'

Fernando paused for a while; then he began again:

'You see I have no village. I live always among strangers, but no evil has come. I left Colombo without a cent, and now I have become rich. What folly to starve where one was born when there are riches to be got in the neighbouring village! Well, I am going now.'

Babun accompanied his guest to the stile of the compound, and took leave of him with the usual words, 'It is well; go and come again.'

Fernando was quite satisfied with his interview. He thought he had gauged Babun, and that he would have no difficulty with him; he seemed so simple and mild. Both the man and woman had obviously been impressed by him and his wealth. He was however, still cautious; he decided to make his first overture through the servant boy, whom he could trust.

The boy was instructed carefully. He was to go to Punchi Menika as if on his own initiative. His master was a rich man, and a great lover of women. He had already remarked upon her beauty. The boy was quite sure that, though his master had not actually said so, he desired her greatly. If she agreed, he would tell his master that the next night that Babun was watching in the chena she would come to his house or would receive him in hers. It would benefit both her and her husband, for his master was very kind and generous.

The attempt was a failure. Punchi Menika listened to what the boy had to say, and then gave him a sound smack in the face, which sent him crying back to his master. She was very angry with the 'badness of these boys from the town,' and she did not suspect that he had been sent by his master.

Fernando beat the servant boy, and himself went to Punchi Menika's compound one evening when he knew that Babun would be watching at the chena.

'Woman,' he said, 'you have beaten my servant boy. Why is that?'

'He came here with evil words, aiya.'

'Evil words? A child of eight?'

'Chi, chi. But he came here with evil words and lies.'

'Lies? What did he say? That your face is very fair, and that all men desire you?'

'Aiya, aiya, do not speak like that. He spoke shameful words. I cannot tell you what he said.'

'Nonsense. You have beaten my servant and you must tell me why, or I must go to the headman.'

'Aiya, why force me to tell what is shameful?'

'What nonsense. Are you a child, then? What shame is there in words?'

'The boy came here with shameful words, saying that you desired a woman. He called me to come to you secretly at night, when my man goes to the chena.'

Fernando looked very hard at Punchi Menika. He smiled when her eyes dropped.

'But what if the boy did not lie? What if he was sent by his master?'

'Hush, aiya. Do not speak like that.'

'Why? Am I so foul that the woman of the villager Babun shrinks from me?'

'It is not that.'

'What is it, then? The women of Colombo and Kamburupitiya have not found me foul. Are you afraid?'

'Yes, aiya, I am afraid.'

'Afraid of what? What harm can come? Who need know? And

what can Babun do? He is a fool. He owes me money. What can he do?'

'I am afraid. It is difficult for me to explain to you, for I see you will grow angry. I am a village woman, ignorant: I am not a woman like that. I went to the man willingly, even against my father's will. He has been the father of my child, that is dead. He is good to me. Let me alone, aiya, let me alone, to keep his house and cook his meals for him as before.'

'Why not? I do not ask you to come to Kamburupitiya to be my wife. There is no talk of leaving your husband. I am rich, and can give you money and jewels. You will bring good fortune to your husband, for I will cancel his debts and give him the share of the other chenas which I promised him.'

'I cannot do it, aiya.'

'What folly! There is nothing to fear. The houses are near with the same fence. No one will know if you come to me through the fence after nightfall. If I say 'Come, I want you,' is it not enough? Do you wish me to lie on the ground before you and pray to you?'

'Enough, enough, aiya. Pardon me, I cannot do it.'

'Will you bring ruin on your man, then?'

'I do not understand.'

'What? She doesn't understand. What cattle these people are! Is Babun in my debt? Is he to get a share of my chenas?'

'Yes, aiya, I heard you tell him so.'

'Well, is anything given for nothing? Do they give you rice in the bazaar for nothing, or kurakkan or cloth? Do they? Fool, why do you stand there looking at me like a buffalo? You – your man, tell him that I have been here, and what I said. Will he sell you to me like a sack of kurakkan? If not, he is a fool too, a dog, a pig; if not, he gets no share of the crop from me, his debts stand and the interest too. I can ruin him. He – I will, too, I will ruin him. Do you hear that? Well, what do you say?'

'What is there to say, aiya? I cannot do it. If this thing must come to us, what can we do? Always evil is coming into this house – from the jungle, my father says. At first there was no

food. Then the devil entered into my father. Then more evil,
upon my sister and her child, and upon my child. The children
died; they killed Punchi Appu; they killed my sister. And now
evil again.'

Punchi Menika had spoken in a very low voice, very slowly.
Fernando stood looking at her. For a moment he was affected by
the resignation and sadness of her tone. Then he thought he had
been a fool to lose his temper and threaten openly. But how
could one deal with cattle like these people? He began to grow
angry again, but he recognised that it was useless and dangerous
further to show his anger and disappointment. He returned
without another word to his house.

His failure astonished him almost more than it annoyed him.
His first thought was to approach Babun himself. Probably the
woman was only frightened of her husband, and probably the
husband would see more clearly the advantages to be gained by
giving his consent. But Fernando had lost a good deal of his
confidence; he felt the need of an advisor and ally. There could
be no danger in consulting the headman. In any case it would be
dangerous for Babehami to oppose him, and there was every
reason to believe that Babehami would be only too glad of an
opportunity of working against Babun and Punchi Menika.

Next day, after he had eaten the evening meal, in the
headman's house, and while he was sitting in the compound
with Babehami, chewing betel, he opened the subject.

'I thought to get your wife's brother to oversee my chenas. He
is a good man, I think.'

Babehami spat. 'What will you pay him?'

'One twentieth of the crop. He is a good man to work.'

'He is a good worker. His chena is always the best, but he is a
fool. He has brought disgrace upon us.'

'Is he married to that woman?'

'No. He went to her father's house and lives there with her.'

'It would be a good thing to take him from them. Is he not
tired of her now?'

'He was mad about her. He would not listen to reason.'

'Ah, but that was at first, long ago. They say the man first finds heaven in a woman, later in a field, and last in the temple. Would you like to get him back to your house?'

'Yes'.

'Well, why not?' Fernando moved nearer to Babehami and lowered his voice. 'Ralahami, I must live here some months. Without a woman what comfort in a house? The woman is not ill-looking and could cook my meals for me. I had thought of this for some days, so I sent my servant boy to her. She answered that she would come, but she was afraid of her man. Then I thought of speaking to the man, but it is not easy for a stranger. I thought, if he marries this woman it is a disgrace to the headman. It is better that his friends speak to him. Probably he is tired of the woman, and will marry from another village some girl who has a dowry of land.'

Babehami seemed to be considering the ground in front of him with great attention; from time to time he spat very deliberately. It was impossible to tell from his face what impression Fernando's suggestion had made upon him. His silence irritated Fernando. 'What swine these villagers are,' he thought.

'Well,' he said at last, 'what do you say?'

'Did she say she would come to you, if Babun allowed her?'

'Yes, but why do you ask that? If the man agrees, what difficulty can there be?'

'Perhaps none, perhaps none, aiya, but who can say? They are mad those people. It happens so sometimes to people who live as we do in the jungle. The spirits of the trees, they say, enter into a family and they are mad and a trouble to the village. Who knows what such people will do?'

'Well?'

'What more is there to say now?'

'Is the plan good?'

'Yes.'

'But will you help me?'

'The plan is a good one certainly. But I am on bad terms with my wife's brother. We quarrelled about the girl. What can I do?'

'If you talk to him now, Ralahami? You quarrelled when he was hot after the girl. That was long ago; and a man soon tires of the woman that has borne him children. And there are many ways, Ralahami, to persuade him if you will help me. There are the debts and the chenas, and many other ways. What is there that a headman cannot do? It is wrong for him to sit still and watch disgrace come upon him and his family. Have you given him his permit to chena yet?'

'No, not yet.'

'Well, you can keep it back. How can they live without chenas? Then there are the courts. I can help you there, for, being of Kamburupitiya, I know the ways of the courts well. There will be cases and trouble for him, and for them.'

Babehami was not to be hurried. He considered the proposal for some minutes. It was the sort of persecution which appealed to him. He would at the same time be injuring those he disliked, helping those in whose debt he stood, and pleasing himself. He could see very little risk in it, and much to gain.

'Well, aiya,' he said at length, 'I will help you if I can. I will speak to Babun. Shall it be done soon?'

'Yes, quickly. Send for him now. There is no harm in doing it before me; and there is no time to lose if I am to get the woman.'

Babehami was at first averse to doing things with such precipitation; he liked to think over carefully each move in his game. But he was overpersuaded by Fernando, who could not restrain his impatience. A message was sent to Babun that the headman wanted to speak to him. Babun was very much astonished at receiving this message, and still more so at his reception. He was given a chew of betel and welcomed warmly.

'Brother,' said the headman, 'it is a bad thing for those of the same blood to quarrel. This Mahatmaya has been speaking of it, saying you are a good man. All that is very long ago, and it is well to forget it.'

'I have forgotten it. I have never had a bad thought of you in my mind, brother.'

'Good, good. Nor I of you, brother, really. Well, and how are things with you now?'

'The light half of the moon returns. This Mahatmaya is giving me his chenas to work for a share of the crop.'

'Good, good. Where there is food, there is happiness. Never have I known a year like this, and I am growing an old man now. On the poya[1] day two months back there was not a kuruni of grain in all the village. I went to the Korala Mahatmaya; I said to him: "Can men live on air?" He is a hard man. He said (his stomach swollen with rice), "For ten years now I have told you to leave your village. There are fields and land elsewhere; there is work elsewhere; they pay for work on the roads. If you make your paddy field on rock, do you expect the rice to grow?" I said to him, "The Government must give food or the people will die." Then he said, "Go away and die quickly," and he abused me, calling me a tom-tom-beater, and drove me away. So I went to this Mahatmaya and arranged about the chenas. Had it not been for him, we should all have starved.'

'I know. The Mahatmaya has been very good.'

'And now again the Mahatmaya said to me: "It is a foolish thing to quarrel with a brother. It is long ago and about a woman. A young man hot after a woman! What use is it? Send for him and be friends."'

'The Mahatmaya is very good to us.'

'I was wrong, brother. I say it to you myself. I used shameful words to you. But that was long ago. A young man must have a woman. It is foolish to stand in his way. Even the buck will turn upon you in the rutting season.'

'All that is forgotten now.'

'So the Mahatmaya says: "It is time," he said, "for him to marry. Send for him and become friends again. For the heat of youth is now past." So I sent for you.'

'I have come.'

'He said to me, "Now is the time. The boy has become a man. When he learns about the woman, he will do as you ask."'

'I do not understand that.'

'The woman has offered to go and live with the Mahatmaya and cook his meals for him. So the Mahatmaya says, "Very well,

---

[1] A poya day is the day of the change of the moon, which is kept as a sacred day by the Buddhist, answering in some ways to the Christian Sunday.

I will take her to live with me while I am here. I will give her food and money, and also to her father. I will give work in my chenas to your brother. So your brother can leave the woman and marry from another village."'

'I do not understand. I do not wish to marry from another village. And what offer of the woman do you talk of?'

'The woman came to the Mahatmaya while you were away in the chena. She offered herself to him. The Mahatmaya said to her, "I cannot take you unless the man gives you." Then he came to me: he said to me, "This woman says this and that to me. It would be better for me to take her to live with me while I am here; and you should marry your brother to an honest woman." So I sent for you.'

'It must be lies, brother. It must be lies. Who told this to you?'

'The Mahatmaya himself. Would he tell lies?'

'Is this true, aiya?' Babun asked Fernando.

'Yes, it is true. The woman came to me.'

'The woman is a whore, brother; I told you so long ago. It is better that you should give her to the Mahatmaya, and marry now from another village. You can come back to my house and live here meanwhile.'

Babun was dazed. His first instinct had been to disbelieve entirely the story about Punchi Menika. He did not believe it now, but he could not disbelieve it. Why should the Mahatmaya lie? He could not tell him to his face that he was lying. He got up and stood hesitating. The others watched him. Fernando had difficulty in repressing his laughter. Several times Babun opened his mouth to speak, and then stopped.

'I do not understand,' he said at last. 'I do not understand this. The woman went to the Mahatmaya? Offered herself? Aiya, that cannot be so. Surely she would be afraid? Yet you yourself say it's true. Aiyo, I do not understand. I must go to the woman herself.'

Babehami got up and caught hold of Babun by the arm, trying to prevent his leaving the compound.

'Do not do that, brother. Let her go, let her go to the

Mahatmaya, and do you stay here. My house is always open to you; stay now and I will tell the woman to go to the Mahatmaya.'

'No, no. I must see her myself.'

'What is the use? There will only be abuse and angry words. It is always lies or foul words in a woman's mouth.'

'I must go, brother. I must see her myself.'

'What folly! But you would never listen to me, and see what has come of it. She is a whore. It was known before, but you would not believe it. You would not listen. Hark, the lizard chirps. It is an evil hour, but again you do not listen. You are going, brother, to meet misfortune.'

Babun allowed himself to be brought back into the compound. His mind worked slowly, and he was dazed by the shock, and by the insinuating stream of the headman's words. But there was a curious obstinacy about him which Babehami recognised and feared. Babun came back, but he did not squat down again. He stood near Fernando; his forehead was wrinkled with perplexity. Surely the story could not be true, and yet how could it be false? Why should the Mahatmaya and Babehami lie to him? The simplicity of his character made him always inclined to believe at once and without question anything said to him. The headman had reckoned on this, and his plan would probably, but for Fernando, have succeeded. Suddenly, however, the latter could no longer restrain his amusement. The wrinkled forehead, the open mouth, the pain and hesitation in Babun's face as he stood before him, seemed to him extraordinarily ridiculous. He laughed. The laugh broke the spell. Babun turned again.

'I must see the woman herself,' he said as he walked away.

'That was foolish, aiya,' said Babehami to Fernando. 'Very foolish. He would have stayed.'

'I know. But I couldn't help it. He stood there like a bull pulled this way and that with a string in its nose. What now?'

'He will come back. Then we shall see. It is spoilt now, I think. This bull is an obstinate brute when it jibs. We may have to use the goad. It will be the only way, I think.'

They waited in silence. The headman proved right. Babun returned. He did not speak to Fernando, but addressed himself to Babehami.

'The Mahatmaya was right to laugh at me for a fool. Yes, I am a fool. I know that. The tale was false. It was the Mahatmaya who called the woman to come to him, and she refused. I knew it. Yes, brother, I knew it. But I was frightened by your words. I thought "he is my sister's man, why should he lie to me?" It was lies. The woman wept for shame when I told her.'

'It was true, brother. It is the woman who is lying now to you. She is frightened of you, frightened that you should know what she has done.'

'I am a fool, brother, but what use is there in repeating lies now? The story was false. It was the Mahatmaya who came to my house and called the woman to him. She refused. She would not leave me.' He turned to Fernando. 'Aiya, why come and trouble us? We are poor and ignorant, and you have wealth, and women in the town as you told us. Leave us in peace, aiya, leave us in peace.'

'It is not lies,' broke in Babehami. 'Truly you are a fool. The woman is ashamed now, and lies to you, and you believe. But what has that to do with it? The Mahatmaya is now ready to take the woman. It is time that this folly should end. Let him take her, and come back to this house.'

'She refuses, I tell you.'

'What has that to do with it? It is time for you to marry, and leave that filth.'

'What is the good, brother, of beginning this again? It will only lead to angry words again. I told you, so many years back, that I want no other wife than this. It is the same now. I will live with no one else. All these lies and words are useless.'

'Ohé, ohé! it may lead to angry words; yes, but are they useless? Last time you refused to listen to me. Well, I did nothing: I allowed you to go your own way. You brought shame on me and my family. I did nothing. I let you go. But now it is different. Suppose they were lies, the words spoken by me just now. They weren't, but suppose they were. What then? The

Mahatmaya wants the woman now. He calls her to him: she will
not come; you refuse to give her. Is it wise, wise brother? Think a
little. Is there much kurakkan in the house after the drought?
The Mahatmaya has made you overseer of his chenas. If the
woman is refused, will you remain overseer? The twentieth of
the crop will go, I think, to some one else. Is it wise for the bull to
fight against the master, when he has the goad in his hand? Is it
wise, too, always to be fighting against the headman? Even the
headman has a little power still. The chena permit has not yet
come for you. Perhaps it may never come. Who knows?'

'The Mahatmaya will not do that – and you – you are my
brother.'

'If the woman is not given to me,' said Fernando, 'neither will
the twentieth be given to you. I have not come here to be laughed
at by cattle like you. First the woman is offered, and then I am
refused! What does it mean? Would you try to make me out a
fool?'

'Very well, aiya, then I will not have the twentieth. The
woman cannot be given to you.'

'Fool,' said Babehami. 'So you refuse again to listen to me?
But remember this time it will not be as it was before. You shall
not always disgrace and insult me.'

'I have never spoken nor thought evil of you, brother. But I tell
you, as I told you before, I will not live without this woman. It is
useless to talk more, for nothing but angry words will follow.
Therefore I am going.'

Babun did not wait for any answer from the two men, but
went quickly from the compound. The other two sat on discuss-
ing the matter for long. They had to take their steps quickly, for
Fernando would only be a few weeks in the village, and he was
very anxious, now that he was really opposed, to possess Punchi
Menika. Their plans were laid that night.

Babun and Silindu very soon became aware of the web that
was being spun around them. They had already begun to
cultivate a chena together: two days after Babun's conversation
with Babehami and Fernando they found another man, Baba
Sinno, a near relation of Babehami, in occupation of it. Babun

went to the headman to inquire what this meant. The headman
was quite ready to explain it. No permit could be given to Babun
and Silindu this year. It was a Government rule that permits
were to be given only to fit persons. Babun and Silindu were not
fit persons, therefore no permits could be given to them. That
was all.

They returned to the compound amazed, overwhelmed.
Babun explained to Silindu the real cause of the headman's act,
the proposal of Fernando and its reception. It was clear that the
two men would stop at nothing, that they had determined upon
the complete ruin of Silindu's family, unless Punchi Menika were
given up. For if no chena were given, it meant starvation; for
they had at the utmost food only for a month, and besides that
nothing but their debts. They saw that Baba Sinno was but a foil;
they did not dare to turn him out by force, because they had no
permits which would give them the right to do so. If they had felt
that there was anyone in the village who would openly take their
part, it would have been different; but they knew that no one
would dare to side with them against the headman and Fernando, who already held the whole village enmeshed in their debt.

The more they discussed it the more horrible became their
fear. In a month they would be starving or forced to leave the
village. There was only one thing for them to do, to put the
whole case before the Assistant Government Agent. Babun set
off for Kamburupitiya next morning with this object. His
trouble and his fear drove him; and he did the three days'
journey in two. On the morning of the third day, hours before
the office opened, he was standing, haggard and frightened, on
the Kachcheri[1] verandah, waiting to fall at the feet of the
Assistant Agent. At last a peon or two arrived, and later some
clerks. At first no one took any notice of him. Then a peon came
and asked him what he wanted. He told him that he had come to
make a complaint to the Assistant Agent. The peon said, 'The
Assistant Agent is away on circuit. You must send a petition.'

'When will he be back?'

[1] Kachcheri is the Government offices.

'I don't know.'

'Where is he now, aiya?'

'I don't know.'

He had not the few cents necessary to buy him a fuller answer. He went from one peon to another, and from one clerk to another trying to learn more particulars. They told him nothing; they did not know, they said, when the Assistant Agent would return, or where he was; he had better have a petition written, and come again a week later. He became stupid with fear and misery. He hung about the verandah hour after hour, doing nothing, and thinking of nothing. At last, late in the afternoon, he wandered aimlessly into the bazaar. He was passing the shop of the Moorman, who had previously made many loans in Beddagama: Cassim, who was sitting within doing nothing, knew Babun and called out to him:

'What are you doing in Kamburupitiya, Babun? Like cotton down in a storm! What is the matter with you? I hear that dog Fernando is in Beddagama – may he die of the fever.'

'I have been to the Kachcheri to lay a complaint before the Agent Hamadoru. The Agent Hamadoru is away on circuit. I cannot learn where he is or when he returns.'

'Ohé! a complaint? Those dogs of peons! Every one knows where the Agent Hamadoru is except the peon; and he only knows when there are fanams in his hand. The Agent Hamadoru is in Galbodapattu on circuit: he will not return for another ten days. Every one knows that.'

'Aiyo! then we are ruined!'

'Why? what is it?'

'We are ruined. Only the Agent Hamadoru could help us, and now it will be too late. Our chena is taken from us. Aiyo! Aiyo!'

'Is this one of Fernando's games? They say that the chenas are his now, and not the Government's. The low caste fisher! Vesige puta! He is a Mudalali now: I expect he hopes to be made the Agent Hamadoru one day.'

'It is he, aiya, he and the headman. They want me to give my wife to the Mudalali. I refused. Now they have taken my chena from me. They will ruin me. The Agent Hamadoru, if he knew, would have interfered to stop this; but now it will be too late by the time I can complain to him. It will be too late, aiya!'

The fat Moorman rolled from side to side with laughter.

'O the dog! O the dog! O the dog! There is no one like these fishers for finding money and women everywhere. Allah! They call us Moormen cunning and clever. The only thing I ever found in Beddagama was bad debts. And here this swine of a fisher finds not only bags of grain, and bags of rupees there, but women too. But I am sorry for you, Babun. I remember you; you were a good man in that accursed village. Come in here now, and I'll see what I can do for you. I should like to stop that swine's game. But it is difficult. One wants time. We must send a petition; the Agent Hamadoru would stop it if he knew. But there are always peons and clerks and headmen in the way before you can get to him. Cents here and cents there, and delays and inquiries! You want time, and we haven't got it. But there is nothing for it but a petition. Here now, I'll write it myself for you to spite that dog Fernando.'

The Mudalali made Babun give him all the particulars, and he wrote the petition, and stamped and posted it. He told Babun to come in again to Kamburupitiya in ten days' time to see him about it. He also gave him food and made him sleep that night in his verandah. The next day Babun, somewhat comforted, set out for his village. He was very weary by the time that he reached it: he felt that he could show little gain from his journey to Silindu and Punchi Menika. Ruin seemed very near to them. They could do little but sit gloomily talking of their fears.

But Babehami and Fernando were meanwhile not idle. The cunning headman and the townman, with his energetic fertile mind, were a strong combination. On the morning after Babun's return to the village a rumour spread through the village that the headman's house had been broken into during the night, and that Babehami had left at once to complain to the Korala. Late in the afternoon of the same day the Korala and Babehami arrived in the village. They called to them three or four of the village men, and went with them straight to Silindu's compound. The Korala, a fat, consequential, bullying man, went in first and summoned Babun, Silindu, and Punchi Menika. They were handed over to Babehami's brother, who was instructed to keep them in the compound, and not to allow them out of his sight.

The news of the burglary had not reached Babun and Silindu. They were bewildered by what was passing. They saw the Korala go into the house with Babehami. They were some time in the house, while the men in the compound talked together in whispers. A little group of men and women had gathered outside the fence, and Fernando stood in the door of his house watching what was happening. At last the two headmen came out of the house. The Korala was carrying a bundle. He walked up to Babun and showed him the bundle: it consisted of two cloths, a pair of gold ear-rings, and some other pieces of gold jewellery.

'Where did you get these from, yakko?'[1] he asked.

'I know nothing about them: they are not mine.'

'Don't lie, yakko. They were in your house. Where did you get them from?'

'Hamadoru, I know nothing about them. Some one must have put them there.'

'Lies. They were stolen last night from the Arachchi's house. The Mudalali saw you leaving the house in the night. Curse you, I shall have to take you into Kamburupitiya now to the court and the magistrate Hamadoru. And what about this fellow?' pointing to Silindu, 'Do you charge him as well?'

'Yes, Mahatmaya,' said Babehami. 'But there is the box too. Should not the jungle round the house be searched for it?'

'Yes. Hi there, you fellows! Go and search that piece of jungle there.'

Three or four men went off slowly and began a desultory search in the jungle which lay behind the compound. Suddenly there was a cry, and one of them lifted up a large box. He brought it to the Korala. The lock had been forced open. It was recognised as the headman's. The case was complete, and the onlookers realised that the evidence against Babun was damning.

---

[1] A term used by superiors to inferiors meaning something like 'fellow.'

Babun and Silindu were taken off to the headman's house. They had to spend the night in the verandah with Babehami's brother, who was there to see that they did not run away. The injustice of this new catastrophe seemed to have completely broken Babun's spirit. His misfortunes were too many and sudden for him to fight against. He refused to talk, and squatted with his back against the wall silent throughout the night. The effect upon Silindu was different. He saw at last the malignity of the headman and how his life had been ruined by it. This last stroke made him aware of the long series of misfortunes, which he now felt were all due to the same cause. This knowledge roused him at last from his resignation and from the torpor habitual to his mind. He talked incessantly in a low voice, sometimes to Babun, but more often apparently to himself.

'They call me a hunter, a vedda? A fine hunter! To be hunted for years now and not to know it! It is the headman who is the vedda, a very clever hunter. I have been lying here like a fat old stag in a thicket while he was crawling, crawling nearer and nearer, round and round, looking for the shot. Where was the watching doe to cry the alarm? Always he shot me down as I lay quiet. But the old hunter should be very careful. In the end misfortune comes. Perhaps this time I am a buffalo, wounded. The wise hunter does not follow up the wounded buffalo, where the jungle is thick. Ha! ha! The wounded buffalo can be as clever as the clever hunter. He hears the man crawling and crawling through the jungle. He stands there out of the track in the shadows, the great black head down, the blood bubbling through the wound, listening to the twigs snap and the dry leaves rustle; and the man comes nearer and nearer. Fool! you cannot see him there, but he can see you now; he will let you pass him, and then out he will dash upon you, and his great horns will crash into your side, and he will fling you backwards through the air as if you were paddy straw. The old buffalo knows, the old buffalo knows; the young men laugh at him, "buffaloes' eyes," they say, "blind eyes, foolish eyes, a foolish face like a buffalo," but he is clever, amma! he is clever – when wounded – when he hears the hunter after him – cleverer than the cleverest hunter.

And when it has gone on for years! all his life! What will he do
then? Will he lie quiet then? Oh! he will lie quiet, yes, and let
them take all from him, daughter and home and food. He will
shake his head and sigh the great sigh, and lie quiet in the mud of
the wallow, very sad. And then at last they come after his life.
Shall they take that too? Then at last he knows and is angry –
very angry – and he stands waiting for them. The fools! They
come on, crawling still; they do not know that he is ready for
them now. The fools! the fools!'

The next morning the Korala took with him the complainant,
the accused, and the witnesses, of whom Fernando turned out to
be one, and started for Kamburupitiya. Punchi Menika went
with them. They travelled slowly, and reached Kamburupitiya on
the fourth morning. Silindu had relapsed into his usual state of
sullen silence; Babun's spirit appeared to be completely broken.
He scarcely understood what the charge against him was; he
knew nothing of why or on what evidence it had been made. He
waited bewildered to see what new misfortune fate and his
enemies would bring upon him.

The parties and witnesses in the case were taken at once to the
court-house. They waited about all the morning on the verandah. The court was a very large oblong room with a roof of flat
red tiles. At one end was the bench, a raised daïs, with a wooden
balustrade round it. There were a table and chair upon the daïs.
In the centre of the room was a large table with chairs round it
for the bar and the more respectable witnesses. At the further
end of the room was the dock, a sort of narrow oblong cage
made of a wooden fence with a gate in it. Silindu and Babun
were locked up in this cage, and a court peon stood by the gate in
charge of them. There was no other furniture in the room except
the witness-box, a small square wooden platform surrounded by
a wooden balustrade on three of its sides.

Nothing happened all the morning: Babun and Silindu squatted down behind the bars of their cage. They were silent: they
had never been in so vast or so high a room. The red tiles of the
roof seemed a very long way above their heads. Outside they
could hear the murmur of the sea, and the rush of the wind, and

the whispered conversation of the witnesses on the verandah; but inside the empty room the silence awed them. About one o'clock there was a stir through the court; the headmen hurried in, a proctor or two came and sat down at the table. The peon nudged Babun and Silindu, and told them to stand up. Then they saw a white Hamadoru, an Englishman, appear on the daïs and sit down. The court interpreter, a Sinhalese Mahatmaya in coat and trousers, stood upon a small wooden step near the bench. The judge spoke to him in an angry voice. The interpreter replied in a soothing deferential tone. The conversation being in English was unintelligible to Babun and Silindu. Then the door of their cage was unlocked, and they were led out and made to stand up against the wall on the left of the bench.

The court-house stood on a bare hill which rose above the town, a small headland which ran out into the sea to form one side of the little bay. The judge, as he sat upon the bench, looked out through the great open doors opposite to him, down upon the blue waters of the bay, the red roofs of the houses, and then the interminable jungle, the grey jungle stretching out to the horizon and the faint line of the hills. And throughout the case this vast view, framed like a picture in the heavy wooden doorway, was continually before the eyes of the accused. Their eyes wandered from the bare room to the boats and the canoes, bobbing up and down in the bay, to the group of little figures on the shore hauling in the great nets under the blazing sun, to the dust storms sweeping over the jungle, miles away where they lived. The air of the court was hot, heavy, oppressive; the voices of those who spoke seemed both to themselves and to the others unreal in the stillness. The murmur of the little waves in the bay, the confused shouts of the fishermen on the shore, the sound of the wind in the trees floated up to them as if from another world.

It was like a dream. They did not understand what exactly was happening. This was 'a case' and they were 'the accused', that was all they knew. The judge looked at them and frowned; this increased their fear and confusion. The judge said something to the interpreter, who asked them their names in an angry threatening voice. Silindu had forgotten what his ge[1] name was; the interpreter became still more angry at this, and Silindu still more sullen and confused. From time to time the judge said a few sharp words in English to the interpreter: Silindu and Babun were never quite certain whether he was or was not speaking to them, or whether, when the interpreter spoke to them in Sinhalese, the words were really his own, or whether he was interpreting what the judge had said.

At last the question of the names was settled. Babehami was told to go into the witness box. As he did so a proctor stood up at the table and said:

'I appear for the complainant, your honour.'

'Any one for the defence?' said the judge.

'Have you a proctor?' the interpreter asked Silindu.

'No,' said Babun, 'we are very poor.'

'No, your worship,' said the interpreter.

Babehami knew exactly what to do; it was not the first time that he had given evidence. He was quite at his ease when he made the affirmation that he would tell the truth, the whole truth, and nothing but the truth. He gave his name and his occupation. Then his proctor stood up and said to him:

'Now Arachchi, tell us exactly what has happened.'

Babehami cleared his throat and then told the following story in a rather sing-song voice:

'About four days ago when I woke up in the morning my wife had gone out into the compound. 'I heard her cry out, "Aiyo, some one has made a hole in the wall of the house." I ran out and saw a hole on the western side of the house. The hole was big enough for a man to crawl through. There are two rooms in the house, one on the eastern side, and one on the western side. We, my wife and I, were sleeping that night in the room on the east side; in the other room was a wooden box in which were clothes and two new sarong cloths and jewellery belonging to my wife. The box was locked. When I saw the hole I ran back

---

[1] Ge is Sinhalese for house. A ge name answers in some respects to a surname.

into the house to see if the box was safe. I found it had disappeared. At that I cried out: "Aiyo, my box has been stolen." Then the Mudalali, who had been staying in the hut next to mine, hearing the cries came up and asked what was the matter. I told him: he said, "Last night about four peyas[1] before dawn I went out into the compound for a call of nature. I heard a noise in your compound. Thinking it was a wild pig I stepped back into the doorway and looked. Then I saw your brother-in-law come running from your compound carrying something in his hands. He ran into the jungle behind his own house." I went straight off to the village of the Korala Mahatmaya; it lies many miles away to the north. Then when the sun was about there (pointing about three-quarters way up the wall of the court) I met the Korala Mahatmaya on the road. The Korala Mahatmaya said, "What are you coming this way for, to trouble me? I am going to Kamburupitiya." I told him what had happened and turned with him to go back. We came to the village in the afternoon. The Korala Mahatmaya went to the accused's house and searched. In the roof between the thatch he found the two sarong cloths and my wife's jewellery, and the box with the lock broken was found in the jungle behind the house.'

When Babehami began his story, Babun and Silindu had not really listened to what he was saying. They were still dazed and confused, they did not quite understand what was going on. But as he proceeded, they gradually grasped what he was doing, and when he told the story about the Mudalali, they saw the whole plot. Their brains worked slowly; they felt they were trapped; there was no way out of it. Babehami's proctor stood up to examine him, but the judge interrupted him:

'The first accused, I understand, is the brother-in-law of the complainant. Is that correct? I propose to charge the accused now. But is there any evidence against the second accused – Silindu, isn't his name? – Mr. Perera?'

The proctor called Babehami to him and had a whispered conversation with him.

---

[1] A peya is a Sinhalese hour, and is equal to about twenty minutes.

'There is no evidence, sir,' he said to the judge, 'to connect him directly with the theft. But he was in the house in which the first accused lived, on the night in question. He must have been an accessory. He is the owner of the house, I understand, and might be charged with receiving.'

'No, certainly not – if that's your only evidence to connect him with the theft. I should not be prepared to convict in any case, Mr. Perera. I shall discharge him at once – especially as the man does not look as if he is quite right in the head.'

'Very well, sir.'

'Charge the first accused only,' said the judge to the interpreter. 'There is no evidence against the second accused. He can go.'

This conversation has been in English and therefore was again unintelligible to the two accused. Their bewilderment was increased therefore when the interpreter said to Silindu, 'You there, go away.' Silindu, not knowing where he had to go, remained where he was. 'Can't you hear, yakko?' shouted the interpreter. 'Clear out.' The peon came up and pushed Silindu out on to the verandah. A small group of idle spectators laughed at him as he came out.

'They'll hang you in the evening, father,' said a small boy.

'I thought the judge Hamadoru said ten years' rigorous imprisonment,' said a young man. Silindu turned to an old man who looked like a villager, and said:

'What does it mean, friend?' Every one laughed.

'You are acquitted,' said the old man; 'go back to your buffaloes.'

Babun also did not understand the acquittal of Silindu. Things appeared to be happening around him as if he were in a dream. The interpreter came and stood in front of him and said the following sentence very fast in Sinhalese:

'You are charged under section 1010 of the Penal Code with housebreaking and theft of a box, clothing, and jewellery, in the house of the complainant, on the night of the 10th instant, and you are called on to show cause why you should not be convicted.'

'I don't understand, Hamadoru.'

'You heard what the complainant said?'

'Yes, Hamadoru.'

'He charges you with the theft. Have you anything to say?'

'I know nothing about this.'

'He says he knows nothing about this,' said the interpreter to the judge.

'Any witnesses?' said the judge.

'Have you any witnesses?' said the interpreter to Babun.

'How can I have witnesses? No one will give evidence against the headman.'

'Any reason for a false charge?' asked the judge.

'Hamadoru, the headman is on very bad terms with me; he is angry with me because of my wife. He is angry with my wife's father. He wanted me to marry from another village. Then he wanted me to give my wife to the Mudalali and because I refused he is angry.'

'Anything else?'

Babun was silent. There was nothing more to say. He looked out through the great doors at the jungle. He tried to think where Beddagama was; but, looking down upon it from that distance, it was impossible to detect any landmark in the unbroken stretch of trees.

'Very well, Mr. Perera,' said the judge.

Mr. Perera got up again and began to examine Babehami.

'How long have you been a headman?'

'Fifteen years.'

'Have you ever had a private case before?'

'No.'

'Are you on bad terms with your brother-in-law?'

'No, but he is on bad terms with me.'

'How is that?'

'There is a Government Order that chenas are only to be given to fit persons. The accused is not a fit person; he could not work, but he is lazy. Therefore chenas were refused to him. He thought that I had done this. It was a Kachcheri Order from the agent, Hamadoru. Last week he was very angry and threatened me because of it. The Mudalali heard him.'

'Is the Mudalali a friend of yours?'

'How could he be, aiya? He is a mahatmaya of Kamburu-pitiya. I am only a village man. How could he be a friend of mine? He comes to the village merely to collect debts due to him.'

'And when he comes, you let him stay in the unoccupied house next to yours. Otherwise you do not know him?'

'Yes, that is true, aiya.'

'Is the Korala related to you?'

'No.'

'A friend of yours?'

'No; he was on bad terms with me. He said I troubled him and was a bad headman.

Mr. Perera sat down.

'Any questions?' said the judge.

'Any questions?' the interpreter asked Babun.

'I don't understand,' said Babun.

'Yakko,' said the interpreter angrily, 'do you want to ask complainant any questions?'

'What questions are there to ask? It is lies what he said.'

There was a pause while the judge waited for Babun to think of a question. The silence confused him, and all the eyes looking at him. He fixed his own eyes on the jungle.

At last Babun thought of a question.

'Did you not ask me to give the woman to the Mudalali?'

'No,' said Babehami.

'Did not the Mudalali call her to go to his house?'

'I know nothing of that.'

'Weren't you angry when I married the woman?'

'No.'

Babun turned desperately to the judge.

'Hamadoru,' he said, 'it is all lies he is saying.' The judge was looking straight at him, but Babun could read nothing in the impassive face; the light eyes, 'the cat's eyes,' of the white Hamadoru frightened him.

'Is that all?' said the judge.

Babun was silent.

'Who is this Mudalali?' said the judge sharply to Babehami.

'Fernando Mudalali, Hamadoru. He comes from Kamburupitiya; he is a trader, he lends money in the village.'

'What's he doing in the village now?'

'He has come to collect debts.'

'When did he come?'

'About a week ago.'

'When is he going?'

'I don't know.'

'Is he married?'

'I don't think so. I don't know.'

'Why do you give him a house to live in?'

'Hamadoru, the little hut was empty. He came to me and said:
"Arachchi," he said, "I must stay here a few days. I want a
house. There is that hut of yours — can I live in it?" So I said,
"Why not?"'

'Whose is the hut?'

'Mine.'

'Why did you build it?'

'It was built, Hamadoru, for this brother-in-law of mine.'

'When?'

'I don't know.'

'What do you mean?'

'Hamadoru, last year, I think.'

'But your brother-in-law lives with his father-in-law?'

'Yes.'

'Then why did you build him a house?'

'There was talk of his leaving the other people.'

'Has the Mudalali ever stayed in the village before?'

'No.'

'Do you owe anything to him?'

'No.'

'Next witness.'

Babehami stood down and the Korala entered the witness-
box. He was examined by Mr. Perera. He told his story very
simply and quietly. He had met Babehami, who had told him
that his house had been broken into and that a box had been

stolen; he described the box and its contents; he suspected his brother-in-law, who had been seen going away from his house in the night, by the Mudalali. The Korala then described how he went into and searched the house, and how he found the cloths and jewellery which answered to Babehami's previous description. He then produced them. The proctor examined him.

'Are you on good terms with the complainant?'

'I am not on good terms or bad terms with him. I only know him as a headman.'

'Do you complain of his troubling you?'

'I complained that he was a bad headman. He has troubled me with silly questions. He is an ignorant man.'

Mr. Perera sat down. 'Any questions?' asked the judge.

'Any questions?' asked the interpreter of Babun.

Babun shook his head. 'What questions are there?' he said.

'Do you know this Mudalali?' said the judge to the Korala.

'I have seen him before in Kamburupitiya.'

'Have you seen him before in Beddagama?'

'No.'

'Did you know that he was there?'

'No.'

'Do you know of any ill-feeling between complainant and accused?'

'No, I did not know the accused at all. I live many miles from Beddagama.'

'Next witness.'

Fernando was the next witness. He wore for the occasion a black European coat, a pink starched shirt, and a white cloth. He was cool and unabashed. He told how he had gone out in the night for a call of nature, how he had heard a noise in the compound of the headman and had then seen Babun come out carrying something and go with it into the jungle behind his own house.

'Could you see what it was?' asked the proctor.

'Not distinctly. He walked as if it were heavy. It was rather large.'

'How did you recognise him? Can you swear it was he?'

'I can swear that it was the accused. I recognised him first by his walk. But I also saw his face in the moonlight.'

'Are you on bad terms with accused? Does he owe you money?'

'I am not on bad terms with him. I scarcely know him. He owes me for kurakkan lent to him. I had arranged to make him my gambaraya. All the villagers there owe me money.'

'How long have you been in the village?'

'About ten days. I am making arrangements for the recovery of my loans. Last crop failed and therefore much is owed to me.'

The proctor sat down.

'Any questions?' said the judge.

'Any questions?' said the interpreter to Babun. Babun shook his head. 'It is lies they are telling,' he murmured.

'Are you married?' the judge asked Fernando.

'No.'

'You live with a woman in Kamburupitiya?'

'Yes.'

'How did you come to settle in the hut in Beddagama?'

I was getting into difficulties with my loans because the crop failed last year. I thought I must go to the village during the chena season and arrange for the repayment. I saw the hut empty there, and went to the headman and asked whether I might live there. He said "Yes."'

'Do you know the accused's wife?'

'I have seen her. Their compound adjoins that of the hut. Otherwise I do not know her.'

'Next witness.'

The man who had found the box gave evidence of how and where he had found it. Various villagers were then called, who identified the things found in Silindu's hut and the box as having belonged to Babehami. They all denied any knowledge of ill-feeling between Babun and the headman or of any intimacy between the headman and Fernando. This closed the case for the prosecution.

The judge then addressed Babun in a speech which was

interpreted to him. Babun should now call any witnesses whom he might have. It was for him to decide whether he would himself go into the witness-box and give evidence. If he gave evidence he would be liable to cross-examination by Babehami's proctor; if he did not, he (the judge) might draw any conclusion from his refusal.

Babun did not really understand what this meant. He did not reply.

'Well?' said the interpreter.

'I don't understand.'

'Are you going to give evidence yourself?'

'As the judge hamadoru likes.'

'Explain it to him properly,' said the judge. 'Now, look here. There is the evidence of the Korala that he found the things in your house. There is no evidence of his being a prejudiced witness. There is the evidence of Fernando that he saw you leaving the complainant's hut at night. You say that Fernando wants your wife, and that the headman is in league with him against you. At present there is no evidence of that at all. According to your story the things must have been deliberately put into your house by complainant, or Fernando – or both. Listen to what I am saying. Have you any witnesses or evidence of all this?'

'Hamadoru, how could I get witnesses of this? No one will give evidence against the headman.'

'I will adjourn the case if you want to call witnesses from the village.'

'What is the good? No one will speak the truth.'

'Well, then, you had better, in any case, give evidence yourself.'

'Get up here,' said the interpreter.

Babun got into the witness-box. He told his story. The judge asked him many questions. Then the proctor began cross examining.

'Are you on bad terms with the Korala? Do you know him well?'

'I am not on bad terms. I scarcely know him.'

'Do you know that Fernando came to the village to recover money, that he has arranged to get the chena crops from many of the villagers in repayment of his loans?'

'Yes.'

'Did he ask you to act as overseer of those chenas and promise you a share of the crop if you did?'

'Yes.'

'Because he thought you the best worker in the village?'

'Yes, I think so.'

'When did this happen?'

'About a week ago.'

The proctor sat down. Babun called no witnesses. There was a curious look of pain and distress in his face. The judge watched him in silence for some minutes, then he told the interpreter to call Silindu. Silindu was pushed into the box, the interpreter recited the words of the affirmation to him. He said, 'I do not understand, Hamadoru.' It took some time to make him understand that he had only to repeat the words after the interpreter. He sighed and looked quickly from side to side like a hunted animal. The eyes of the judge frightened him. He was uncertain whether he was being charged again with the theft. He had not listened to what was going on after he had been sent out of the court. It occurred vaguely to him that the best thing would be to pretend to be completely ignorant of everything. He still thought of the wounded buffalo listening to the hunter crawling after him through the scrub: 'He doesn't move,' he muttered to himself, 'until he is sure: he stands quite stupid and still, listening always; but when he sees clear, then out he rushes charging.'

'Stop that muttering,' said the judge, 'and listen carefully to what I ask you. You've got to speak the truth. There's no charge against you; you've got nothing to fear if you speak the truth. Do you understand?'

'I understand, Hamadoru,' said Silindu. But he thought, 'They are cunning hunters. They lie still in the undergrowth, waiting for the old bull to move. But he knows: he stands quite still.'

'Is there any reason why the headman should bring a false case against you and the accused?'

'I don't know, Hamadoru.'

'You are not on bad terms with him personally.'

'I have nothing against him. He does not like me, they say.'

'Why doesn't he like you?'

'Hamadoru, how should I know that?'

'You have never had any quarrel with him?'

'No, Hamadoru.'

'Are you related to him?'

'I married a cousin of his wife.'

'The accused lives in your house? He is married to your daughter?'

'Yes, Hamadoru.'

'Do you know of any quarrel between him and the headman?'

'How should I know that?'

'There was no quarrel at the time of the marriage?'

'They say this and that, but how should I know, Hamadoru?'

'You know nothing about it yourself, then?'

'No, Hamadoru.'

'Do you know the Mudalali Fernando?'

'No, Hamadoru.'

'You don't know him? Doesn't he stay in the hut adjoining your compound?'

'I have seen him there. I have never spoken with him.'

'Did you hear of anything between him and your daughter?'

'They talk, Hamadoru.'

'What did they say?'

'They said he wanted my daughter.'

'Who said? When?

'This man' (pointing to Babun).

'When?'

'Three or four days ago.'

'You know nothing more, yourself, about this?'

'No, Hamadoru.'

Neither Babun nor Babehami's proctor asked Silindu any questions; he was told to go away, and was pushed out of court by the peon. The case was over, only the judgment had to be delivered now. The judge leant back in his chair, gazing over the jungle at the distant hills. There was not a sound in the court. Outside, down on the shore, the net had been hauled in, and the fish sold. Not a living thing could be seen now, except an old fisherman sitting by a broken canoe, and looking out over the waters of the bay. The wind had died away, and sea and jungle lay still and silent under the afternoon sun. The court seemed very small now, suspended over this vast and soundless world of water and trees. Babun became very afraid in the silence. The judge began to write; no one else moved, and the only sound in the world seemed to be the scratching of the pen upon the paper. At last the judge stopped writing. He looked at Babun, and began to read out his judgment in a casual, indifferent voice, as if in some way it had nothing to do with him. The interpreter translated it sentence by sentence to Babun.

'There is almost certainly something behind this case which has not come out. There is, I feel, some ill-feeling between complainant and accused. The complainant impressed me most unfavourably. But the facts have to be considered. There can be no doubt that complainant's things were found hidden in the house in which accused lives, and that the box was found in the jungle behind the house. The evidence of the Korala is obviously trustworthy on these points. There is clear evidence, too, that a hole had been made in complainant's house wall. Then there is the evidence of the Mudalali. As matters stand, it was for the accused to show that the evidence was untrustworthy. He has not really attempted to do this. His father-in-law's evidence, if anything, goes to show that there is nothing in complainant's story that Fernando wanted to get hold of his wife. Accused's defence implies that there was a deliberate conspiracy against him. I cannot accept his mere statement that such a conspiracy existed without any corroborating evidence of motive for it. He has no such evidence. Even if there were ill-feeling over the refusal of a chena or something else, it would cut both ways; that is, it might have been accused's motive for the theft. I convict accused, and sentence him to six months' rigorous imprisonment.'

Babun had not understood a word of the broken sentences of the judgment until the interpreter came to the last words, 'six months' rigorous imprisonment.' Even then, it was only when the peon took hold of him by the arm to put him back again into the cage, that he realised what it meant – that he was to be sent to prison.

'Hamadoru,' he burst out, 'I have not done this. I cannot go to prison, Hamadoru! It is all lies, it is lies that he has said. He is angry with me. I have not done this. I swear on the Beragama temple I have not done this. I cannot go to prison. There is the woman, Hamadoru, what will become of her? Oh! I have not done this. I have not.'

The proctors and idlers smiled; the peon and the interpreter told Babun to hold his tongue. The judge got up and turned to leave the court.

'I am sorry,' he said, 'but the decision has been given. I treated you very leniently as a first offender.'

Every one stood up in silence as the judge left the court. As soon as he had left, everything became confusion. Proctors, witnesses, court officials, and spectators all began talking at once.

Babun crouched down moaning in the cage. Punchi Menika began to shriek on the verandah, until the peon came out and drove her away. Only Silindu maintained his sullenness and calmness. He followed Babun when he was taken away by the peon to the lock-up. At one point, when he saw that the peon was not looking, he laid his hand on Babun's arm and whispered:

'It is all right, son, it is all right. Don't be afraid. The old buffalo is cunning still. Very soon he will charge.' He smiled and nodded at Babun, and then left him to find Punchi Menika.

It took some time for Silindu to find Punchi Menika. She had wandered aimlessly away from the court through the bazaar. Silindu was now extraordinarily excited, he seemed to be almost happy. He ran up to her, took her by the hand, and began leading her quickly away out of the town.

'We must go away at once,' he said. 'There is much to think of and much to do. It is late, but we at least do not fear the jungle. The jungle is better than the town. We can sleep by the big trees at the second hill.'

'But, Appochchi, my man. What will become of him? What will they do to him? Will they kill him?'

'Babun is all right. I have told him. The Government do not kill. There is no killing here. But in the jungle, always killing – the leopard and jackal, and the hunter. Yes, and the hunter, always killing, the blood of deer and pig and buffalo. And at last, the hunting of the hunter, very slow, very quiet, very cunning; and at the end, after a long time, the blood of the hunter.'

'But, Appochchi, stop, do. What does it mean? They are taking him to prison. What will they do with him? Shall we never see him again?'

'The hunter? Yes, yes we shall see him again. Very soon, but he will not see us?'

'What is this about the hunter? It is my man I am talking about.'

'Oh, Babun. He is all right. The white Hamadoru said, "Six months' rigorous imprisonment." I heard that quite clear at the end. "Six months' rigorous imprisonment." It was all that I heard clearly. He is all right. There is no need for you to cry. They will take him away over there – (Silindu pointed to the east) – there is a great house – I remember I saw it a long time ago when I went on a pilgrimage with my mother. They will put him in the great house, and give him rice to eat, so I hear. Then he will come back to the village – but it will be after the hunting."

'O Appochchi, are you sure?'

'Yes, child, all will be well after the hunting. But now I must think.'

Punchi Menika saw that it would be impossible to get anything more out of Silindu in his present state. They walked on in silence. As they walked his excitement began to die down. He seemed to be thinking deeply. From time to time he muttered to himself. Late in the evening they came to the big trees. Silindu collected some sticks and made a fire. Then he squatted down while Punchi Menika cooked some food which they had carried with them.

Once or twice as they sat round the fire, after having eaten the food, Punchi Menika began to question Silindu about Babun, but he did not reply; he did not seem to hear her. Her mind was numbed by the fear and uncertainty. She lay down on the ground, and an uneasy sleep came to her. Suddenly she was aroused by Silindu shaking her. She saw in the light of the fire how his face was working with excitement.

'Child, there are two of them, two of them the whole time, and I never saw it.'

'What do you mean? Where?'

'Hunting me, child, hunting us all – me, you, and Babun, and Hinnihami. They killed Hinnihami, your sister. I found her lying there in the jungle, dying. They did that. But they shall not get you. There are two of them. Listen! I hear them crawling round us in the jungle, do you hear? Now – there ——! I thought there was only one, fool that I was – the little headman. But now I hear them both. The little headman first and then the other; the man with the smooth black face and the smile. It was he, wasn't it? Didn't Babun say so? He came to you and called you to come to his house. Babun said so, I heard him. Fernando – the Mudalali – he wanted to take you away, but he couldn't. Then he went to the headman and together they went to hunt us. Isn't that true? Isn't that true?'

'Yes, Appochchi, yes. It was because they wanted me for the Mudalali. Then they took the chena away and then they brought the case. They have taken my man from me, what shall I do?'

'Hush, I am here. They shall do no more. Listen, child. It is true that they have taken Babun from you. For six months he will be over there. "Very well," they think. They thought to send me there too, but the judge Hamadoru was wise. "Get out," he said to me. I did not understand then, and they laughed at me, but I understand now. Well, those two will come back to the village. "The man," they think, "is away over there for six months, only the woman and the mad father are here. What can they do? The Mudalali can now take the woman." Is this true?'

'Appochchi! It is what I fear. It is true.'

'It is true. But do not be afraid. The old father is there, but he is not altogether mad. The Mudalali will come back to-morrow, perhaps, or the next day, with the headman. Then they will begin again.'

'Yes, yes. That is what I fear, Appochchi. What can we do? we must go away.'

'Hush, child. Do not cry out. There is no need to be afraid. We cannot go away. How can we live away from the village and the jungle which we know. That is foolish talk. There in the town I do not understand even what they say to me; and the noise and the talking in the bazaar, and people always laughing, and the long hard roads and so many houses all together! How could we live there? But in the village I am not altogether mad. It is folly to talk of leaving it and the jungle. Very soon I shall feel the gun in my hand again. Then I shall be a man again, slipping between the trees — very quietly. Ha, ha! we know the tracks, little Arachchi. I remember, child, when I was but a boy, I went out once with my father for skins and horns. He was a good hunter and knew the jungle well. We went on and on — many days — round and round too — he leading, and I following. And at last we came to very thick jungle which not even he knew. And a sort of madness came on us to go on and on always, and we had forgotten the village and the wife and mother. The jungle was tall, dense, and dark, and the sky was covered with cloud — day after day — so that one could not tell the west from the east. And at last, when we had many skins and horns, my father stopped, and stood still in the track and laughed. "Child," he said, "we are mad, we have become like the bear and the elephant; it is time to return to the village." Then he turned round and began to walk. Soon he stopped again, frowning. It was very dark. He stood there for a little, thinking; and then climbed a very big tree and looked around for a long time. Then he came down and I saw from his face that he was very afraid. We said nothing, but started off again. For many peyas we walked and always through very thick jungle. Again he stopped and climbed a tree and again, when he came down, there was great fear in his face.

Aiyo! that was the first time that I saw the fear, the real fear of the jungle; but then I did not understand. "Appochchi," I said, "what is the matter?" "Boy," he said, and his voice trembled; "we are lost. I do not know where we are, nor where the village lies, nor how we came, nor which is east and which is west. From the trees I can see nothing which I know, not even the hill at Beragama, only the tops of the trees everywhere. Therefore we must be very far from the village. I have heard of such things happening to very good hunters; but always before I have known the way. Punchi Appu must have died like that. Wandering on and on until no powder is left and no food. Aiyo! the jungle will take us, as they say." Then I said, "Appochchi, do not be afraid. I do not know which way we came, and I cannot tell just now which is west and which is east because of the clouds; but I know where the village lies. It is over there." "Can you lead the way?" he asked, and I said, "Yes." Then he said, "Perhaps you know, perhaps you do not; but now one way is as good as another for me. You go first." At that I was pleased, and led on straight to where I knew the village must lie. For two days I led the way and my father said nothing, but I saw that he became more and more afraid. And on the third day, suddenly he cried out, "I know this: this track leads to the village. You are going right." It was a track I had never been on, but I still led the way; and on the fourth day we entered the village — well, what was I saying? Yes, I know the tracks, even in those days when I was a boy I knew the jungle. But this time it requires clever hunting.'

'Yes, Appochchi, but what to do now, when they come back to the village?'

'Those two! Ah! now you listen, child. I have thought over it all this time and there is only one way. I shall kill them both.'

'Kill them! O Appochchi, no, no. You are mad.'

'Am I mad? And what if I am? Haven't they always called me mad, the mad vedda. Well, now let them see if I am mad or not. Have they not hunted me for all these years and am I always to go running like a stupid deer through the jungle? No, no, little Arachchi; no, no. This time it is the old wounded buffalo. Three times, four times that night in the hut when I saw it first I got up to get my gun and end it. And again, after the court, I would have done it, had I had a gun. But I thought – no, not yet, for once we must act cunningly, not in anger only. The buffalo's eye is red with anger, but he stands quiet until the hunter has passed. Then he charges.'

'But, Appochchi, you must not say that. You cannot do it. You must come away. They will take you and hang you.'

'What can I do? I cannot leave the village; I will not; I have told you that. There is no other way.'

'But what are you going to do?'

'Ah! I must think. It needs cunning and skill first. I must think.'

'No, no, Appochchi; no, no. It would be better to give me to the Mudalali!'

'I would rather kill you than that. Do you hear? I shall kill you if you go to the Mudalali.'

'Oh! oh! isn't it enough that they should have taken my man from me? And now more evil comes.'

'I tell you that I will end this now. Now I shall sleep and to-morrow think of the way.'

Silindu refused to listen any further to Punchi Menika's expostulations. He lay down by the fire and soon slept. Next day, and throughout their journey to the village, he was very silent, and refused to discuss the subject at all with her. The lethargy habitual to him had left him completely. He was in an extraordinary state of excitement, goaded on perpetually by great gusts of anger against Babehami and Fernando. When he got back to his house he sat down in the compound in a place from which he could see the headman's house, and waited. He watched the house all day, and, when in the evening he saw the headman return, he smiled. Then he got up and went into the hut. He took his gun which stood in the corner of the room, unloaded it, and reloaded it again with fresh powder and several big slugs. He examined the caps carefully, chose two, and put them in the fold of his cloth. Then he lay down and slept.

Next morning he was very quiet and thoughtful; but if any one had watched him closely, he would have seen that he was really in a state of intense excitement. After eating the morning meal he took his gun and went over to the headman's house. To the astonishment of Babehami and his wife he walked into the house, put his gun in the corner of the room, and squatted down. Babehami watched him closely for a minute or two; he felt uneasy; he noted that the curious wild look in Silindu's eyes was greater than ever.

'Well, Silindu, what is it?' he said.

'Arachchi, I have come to you about this chena. I cannot live without chena. You must give it back to me.'

'You heard in the court that the chena cannot be given to you. It has been given to Appu. Let us have an end of all this trouble.'

'Yes, Arachchi, that is why I have come to you. I want an end of all this trouble. Do you hear that? An end now – to-day – of trouble. Trouble, trouble, for years. We must end it to-day. Do you hear?'

'What do you mean?'

'Yes. What did I say? This, this. Now, Arachchi, that was nothing; do not mind what I said then. I was thinking, thinking. You know they call me mad in the village. Well, I was thinking, you know, now that Babun is over there for six months, I heard the judge Hamadoru say that clearly, but to me he said merely, "Clear out" – I was never a friend of that Babun – all the trouble has come from him – he took Punchi Menika from me, and then Hinnihami. I saw her lying in the jungle by the deer – what did we call him? Kalu Appu? Punchi Appu? Yes, yes, Punchi Appu, that was long ago. They beat her. They threw stones at her. That was long ago – in the jungle. But now Babun is away for six months. When he comes back, I shall say to him, "Clear out," as the judge Hamadoru said. They laughed at me then. A foolish old man, a mad old man, eh? Ha, ha! little Arachchi, little Arachchi, you have laughed at me too – for years, haven't you, haven't you?'

'What is all this, Silindu? What do you mean? I don't understand.'

'Ah, Arachchi, it is nothing. Do not mind what I say. I do not know what I was saying. I am a poor man, Arachchi, very ignorant, a little mad. But I am a quiet man; I have given no trouble in the village. You know that well, Arachchi, don't you? I cannot speak well – like you, Arachchi – in the court. But this is what I want to say. I do not like this Babun; all the trouble has come from him. I am a quiet man in the village, you know that. I said to my daughter on the way here by the big palu-trees at the second hill – I said to her, "The man is now sent away; he will be over there for six months. He is a foolish man. It is he who has brought the trouble. The Mudalali is a good man. The Arachchi, too, is a good man. Why should we quarrel with those two? There is no shame in your going to the Mudalali." Then my daughter said, "I will do as you think best, Appochchi." Do you understand now, Arachchi?'

Silindu stopped. The Arachchi had been watching him narrowly. He began to understand the drift of Silindu's incoherent words. But he still felt uneasy. As Silindu spoke, his suppressed excitement became more and more apparent in his voice and words. But Babehami knew well that he was mad, and that he was also wonderfully stupid. It was just like him to do things in this wild way. The more Babehami thought of it, the more he became convinced that the conviction of Babun had done its work. Silindu and Punchi Menika had given in.

'Yes, I think I understand,' he said. 'It is true that the Mudalali will take your daughter. He is a good man; and the trouble came from Babun, as you say.'

'That is it, Arachchi, that is it. Let the Mudalali take Punchi Menika. My daughter cannot live with thieves now. She will go to the Mudalali. Do you understand?'

'Yes, Silindu. But it must be done quietly. She cannot go openly to his house, or there will be silly talk, after what was said in the court.'

'No, no. It must be done quietly, very quietly.'

'I will tell the Mudalali, and she can come at night to him. Afterwards, perhaps, she can live at the house; but at first she must go secretly at night.'

'Ha, ha, Arachchi. You are clever! How clever you are! You think of all things. Yes, it must be all done quietly, quietly.'

'Very well, Silindu, I will tell the Mudalali. It is a good thing to end all this trouble, like this.'

'Yes, it is a very good thing to end it – like this. Yes – like this, like this. But now the chena, Arachchi. I cannot live without the chena. Without a chena I must starve. You cannot see me starve. Even now there is no grain in my house. You must give me the chena.'

Babehami thought for a while, then he said:

'Well, I will see what can be done; perhaps I can arrange with Appu about the chena. We will see.'

'Yes, Arachchi, but let us have done with it once and for all. The thing is settled. Appu cannot be left there. Come.'

'Why, what do you want? Don't you trust me?'

'Yes, I trust you – why not, Arachchi? – but I am afraid of Appu. If he is left there to do work, he will refuse to go. He is in the chena now. It would be better to go and tell him at once.'

'I cannot go now. To-morrow, perhaps.'

'Arachchi, it is but two miles. You said it is a good thing to end the trouble. Let us settle it now, to-day, and the Mudalali can have Punchi Menika to-night.'

Babehami was silent. He disliked being hurried. On the other hand he would be very glad to see the whole matter settled. His action with regard to the chena troubled him because it was dangerous. He knew that the petition had been presented, and he was not at all sure that he would come off as well in an inquiry as he had in the court. It would also be wise to bind Silindu to him by giving him back the chena, and not to risk his changing his mind about the Mudalali and Punchi Menika. He argued a little more, and stood out half-heartedly against Silindu's urgings to start at once. At last he gave in, and they started for the chena.

They followed a narrow jungle track which had been lately cleared. The tangle of shrubs and undergrowth and trees was like a wall on each side of the track. The headman walked first, and Silindu, carrying his gun, followed. For the first three-quarters of a mile they walked in silence, except for a word or two which the head man shouted back to Silindu without turning his head. Silindu had fallen somewhat behind; he quickened his pace, and came up close to the headman; he was muttering to himself.

'What do you say?' asked Babehami.

'What? Was I talking? I do not know, Arachchi. They say the hunter talks to himself in the jungle. It is a custom. Have you ever been a hunter, Arachchi?'

'No. You know that well enough.'

'Oh yes. You are no hunter. Who should know that better than I? But do they call me a good hunter, Arachchi? skilful, cunning? Do I know the tracks, Arachchi?'

'Of course, every one knows you to be the best hunter in the district.'

'Aiyo, the best hunter in the district! And do you know, Arachchi, that I am afraid of the jungle?'

'So they say. What are you afraid of?'

Silindu began to speak with great excitement. As he went on his voice began to get shriller and shriller; it trembled with anger and fear and passion.

'I am afraid of everything, Arachchi; the jungle, the devils, the darkness. But, above all, of being hunted. Have you ever been hunted, Arachchi? No, of course you are not a hunter, and therefore have never been hunted. But I know. It happens sometimes to the cleverest of us. The elephant, they say; but that I have never seen. But the buffalo; I have seen that – here – on this very track – before it was cleared – many years ago. The buffalo is stupid, isn't he, little Arachchi? Very stupid; he does not see – he does not hear – he goes on wallowing in his mud. And they hunt him year after year – year after year – he does not know – he does not see them – he does not hear them. Do you know that? I know it – I am a hunter. Then – then having crept close, they shoot him. It was near here. At first, crash – he tears away through the jungle, the blood flowing down his side. He is afraid, very afraid – and in pain. But the pain brings anger, and with anger, anger, Arachchi, comes cunning. And now, Arachchi, now comes the game, the dangerous game. The young men laugh at it, but the wise hunter would be afraid. There he stood, do you see? – there – under that maiyilittan-tree, head down, very still. And the hunter – fool, fool – crept after him through the undergrowth: there was no track then. Ah, it was thick then: he could not see anything but the shrubs and thorns; he did not see the red eyes behind him nor the great head down. For the other was cunning now, cunning, and very angry. And when the hunter had gone on a little – just where you are now, Arachchi – then – do you hear, little Arachchi? – then, out and crash, he charged, charged, like this ——'

Babehami had at first hardly listened, but the fury and excitement of Silindu had at last forced his attention. As Silindu said the last words, Babehami half stopped and turned his head: he just saw Silindu's blazing eyes and foam on the corner of his lips: at the same moment he felt the cold muzzle of the gun pressed against his back. Silindu pulled the trigger and Babehami fell forward on his face. A great hole was blown in the back, and the skin round it was blackened and burnt; the chest was shattered by the slugs which tore their way through. The body writhed and twisted on the ground for a minute, and then was still. Silindu kicked it with his foot to see whether it was dead. There was no movement. He reloaded his gun and turned back towards the village. His excitement had died down: the old lethargy was coming upon him again. He felt this himself and walked faster, muttering, 'Even now it is not safe. There were two of them. There is still the other.'

When Silindu got back to the village, Fernando was in the headman's compound. When he saw Silindu he came down towards the fence and called out to him, 'Where is the Arachchi? They say he went out with you.' Silindu walked up towards the stile, and stopping levelled his gun at the Mudalali. Fernando stepped back, his mouth wide open, his eyes staring, his whole face contorted with fear. He cowered down behind the stile, stretching his hands vaguely out between the wooden bars, and shouted:

'Don't shoot! don't shoot!'

The stile was little or no protection: between the two bottom bars Silindu could see the Mudalali's fat stomach and legs. He took careful aim between the bars and fired. Fernando fell

backwards, writhing and screaming with pain. Silindu went and
looked over the stile: at the same moment Babehami's wife
rushed out of the house. But he saw that his work had been
accomplished; blood was pouring from the Mudalali's stomach;
his two legs and one of his hands were shattered. 'The trouble is
ended,' he muttered.

He walked very slowly to his house. He put the gun in the
corner of the room, thought for a minute, and then immediately
left the hut. He saw that already there was a crowd of people in
the headman's compound: the women were screaming. Silindu
turned into the jungle at the back of his house, and walking
quickly cut across to the track which led to Kamburupitiya.

CHAPTER VIII

BEFORE Silindu reached the Kamburupitiya track, he stopped and squatted down with his back against a tree. He wanted to think. After the wild excitement which had possessed him now for three days, a feeling of immense lassitude came upon him. His mind worked slowly, confusedly; he had no clear idea of where he was going, or of what he ought to do. He was very tired, very unhappy now; but he felt no regret for what he had done — no remorse for the blood of the Arachchi and of Fernando could trouble him. So far as they were concerned, he only felt a great relief.

He wanted to lie down and sleep. He leant back against the tree and began to doze, but he started up again immediately, listening for footsteps of pursuers. His first idea had been simply to run away into the jungle, to get away at any rate from the village. The hunt would begin; he would be hunted once again, he knew that. Then he thought of going east where the thick jungle stretched unbroken for miles. He could live there in some cave among the rocks; he could live there safe from his hunters for months. He had heard stories of other men doing this: strange men from other districts, whom the Government and the police were hunting down for some crime. They came down from the north, so it was said, flying to the sanctuary of the uninhabited jungle where they lay hidden for years; they lived alone in caves and in trees, eating leaves and wild fruit and honey, and the birds and animals which they managed to snare or kill. They were never caught; there were no villages in that wilderness from which information could come to the police. Sometimes one of the few bold hunters, who were the only people to penetrate these solitudes, would catch a glimpse of a wild, naked man in a cave or among the shadows of the trees. Some of them perhaps eventually, trusting to the lapse of time and to the short memory of the Government, went back to their villages and their homes.

But most of them died of fever in the jungle to which they had fled.

If such a life were possible for men from distant villages, who did not know the jungle, it would be easy for Silindu. But as he squatted under the trees thinking of what he should do, a feeling of horror for such a life crept over him, and his repugnance to flying became stronger and stronger. He was very tired. What he desired – and the desire was sharp – was to rest, to be left alone untroubled in the village – in his hut, in his compound – to sleep quietly there at night, to sit hour after hour through the hot day under the mustard-tree in the compound. But in the jungle there would be no rest. It was just in order to escape the terror – the feeling of the hunted animal, the feeling that some one was always after him meaning evil – that he had killed the Arachchi and the Mudalali. And if he fled into the jungle now, he would have gained nothing by the killing. He would live with that feeling for months, for years, perhaps for ever. The hunt would begin again, and again it was he who would be the hunted.

Then he thought of returning to the village, but that too would be useless; he would get no peace there. He knew well what would happen. The Korala would be sent for; he would be seized, worried, bullied, ill-treated probably. That would be worse than the jungle. Suddenly the conviction came to him that it would be best to end it all at once, to go into Kamburupitiya and give himself up to the Ratemahatmaya and the white Hamadoru, to confess what he had done. He got up and started for the town immediately, keeping to the game tracks in the thick jungle, and avoiding the main tracks, for he did not wish to meet any one.

He walked slowly, following instinctively the tangled winding tracks. His lassitude and fatigue increased. He reached Kamburu-pitiya in the evening of the third day, and asked his way to the Ratemahatmaya's house.

When Silindu reached the Ratemahatmaya's house, no news of the murder had yet come to Kamburupitiya. He had walked slowly, but what was a slow pace for him was faster than that of the other villagers. He went into the compound, and walked cautiously round the house: in the verandah through the lattice-work he saw the Ratemahatmaya lying in a long chair. There was a table with a lamp upon it beside him. Silindu coughed. The Ratemahatmaya looked up and said sharply:

'Who is there?'

'Hamadoru, it is I. May I come into the verandah?'

'What do you want at this time? Come to-morrow. I can't attend to anything tonight.'

'Hamadoru, I come from Beddagama. There has been a murder there.'

'Come in, then.'

Silindu came into the verandah and salaamed. He stood in front of the Ratemahatmaya.

'Hamadoru,' he said, 'I have killed the Arachchi and the Mudalali.'

The Ratemahatmaya sat up. 'You? What? What do you mean? Who are you?'

'I am Silindu of Beddagama. The Arachchi brought a false case against me and my son-in-law. May I sit down, Hamadoru? I am very tired. Babun was sent to prison by the judge Hamadoru, but to me, he said, "Clear out." The case was false. They were trying to bring evil upon me and my daughter. The Mudalali wanted the girl. They were still trying to bring evil on me, so I said, "Enough." I took the gun and I went out with the Arachchi over there to the chena, and I shot him through the back. He is dead, lying there on the track. Then I went back to the village and shot the Mudalali in the belly through the stile. He was not dead then, but I looked over and saw the blood coming fast from the belly low down. He must be dead now.'

The Ratemahatmaya was not a brave man. As he listened to Silindu's short expressionless sentences, the bald description of the shedding of blood, given in the tired voice of the villager, he became afraid. He sat up in his chair looking at Silindu, who crouched in front of him, motionless, watching him. The light of the lamp fell upon the dark, livid face. It was the face of the grey monkeys which leap above the jungle among the tree-tops, and peer down at you through the branches; a face scarred and pinched by suffering and weariness and fear. It was as if something evil from the darkness, which he did not understand, had suddenly appeared in his quiet verandah. He looked out nervously over Silindu's head into the night: the light of lamp in the verandah made it seem very dark outside. The Ratemahat-maya became still more afraid in the silence which followed Silindu's speech. He suddenly got up and shouted for his servant. There was the sound of movements in the back of the house, and a dirty servant boy, in a dirty vest and cloth, came blinking and yawning into the verandah. The Ratemahatmaya told him to stand by Silindu.

The Ratemahatmaya drew in a deep breath of relief. The beating of his heart became quieter.

'Now, yakko!' he said in a sharp angry tone, 'stand up.'

Silindu did not move; he looked up at the Ratemahatmaya with weary eyes and said, 'Hamadoru! I am very tired. For days now there has been no rest for me. Aiyo! I cannot remember how long it is now since I sat quiet in my compound. Let me sleep now. I have come straight to you and told you all. I thought at first I would run away. I could have lived out there for months, and you would not have caught me. But I was tired of all this: I am very tired. I thought: No. What is the good? Out there away from the village, and the hut, and the compound, and the daughter? It is the evil all over again. Aiyo! how tired I am of it. It is better to end it now. So I came here. I have told you no lies. What harm can I do now? Let me sleep here, and to-morrow you can do what you like to me.'

'Do you hear what I say? Stand up, yakko, stand up. Make him stand up.'

The servant boy kicked Silindu in the ribs, and told him to stand up. Silindu rose slowly.

'Now, then. You say you have killed the Arachchi and the Mudalali. Is that Fernando, the boutique-keeper?'

'Yes, Hamadoru, yes. Fernando, the boutique-keeper.'

'Fetch me ink and paper and a pen.'

The servant boy fetched the paper, ink, and pen. Meanwhile

Silindu again squatted down. The Ratemahatmaya prepared to write.

'Didn't you hear me tell you to get up? Get up, yakko' (the servant boy kicked Silindu again). 'Now, then. When did you kill them, and how?'

'Three or four days ago. It was in the morning. I went with the Arachchi to the chena. I shot him through the back.'

'Where did you get the gun?'

'It was my gun. I had it in my house.'

'Was it licensed?'

'Yes, Hamadoru. I am very tired. What is the good of all these questions? I tell you I killed them both. Let me be. I cannot think of these things now. To-morrow, perhaps, to-morrow. Surely you have me here safe, and can do with me what you like to-morrow.'

The Ratemahatmaya was a self-important, fussy little man; he was also timid, and not fond of taking responsibilities. The sudden appearance of Silindu with this strange story out of the darkness had upset him. He was very annoyed when Silindu again sank down into a squatting position. 'Stand up, fellow,' he said. 'Stand up. Didn't you hear me, pariah? Stand up. You've got to answer my questions. Now, then. What did I ask last? Now, then——'He paused and thought for a moment. 'It is not, perhaps, too late. Perhaps I had better take him at once to the magistrate. Yes, that's better. You there get the bull put into the hackery. No, no, stop there; you must look after the man. Keep him there. Kalu Appu! Kalu Appu! Call Kalu Appu! Kalu Appu! Hoi! D'you hear? Wake up! Put the bull in the hackery and hurry up.'

At last another servant boy was woken up, the bull was put into the hackery. The Ratemahatmaya put on a dark coat, and, with many curses and complaints, got into the cart. Silindu followed slowly with the servant boy. They trailed wearily along the dark roads for three-quarters of a mile: then the cart stopped in the compound of the magistrate's bungalow. The Ratemahatmaya got out and went round to the back of the house to announce his arrival through the servants. Silindu squatted down near the hackery; he was no longer quite conscious of what was going on around him; after a while the Ratemahat-maya called to him to come round into the house, and the boy who had driven the bullock poked him up with the goad.

He was taken along a broad dark verandah, and suddenly found himself in a large well-lit room. Had it not been for the stupor of his fatigue he would have been very frightened, for he had never seen anything like this room before. It seemed to him to be full of furniture, and all the furniture to be covered with strange objects. In reality there was only a little travel-battered furniture in the barn-like white-washed room. There was matting on the floor, and rugs on the matting. An immense writing-table littered with letters and papers stood in front of the window. There were three or four tables on which were some ugly ornaments, mostly chipped or broken, and a great many spotted and faded photographs. A gun, a rifle, and several sentimental pictures broke the monotony of the white walls. The rest of the furniture consisted of a great many chairs, two or three lamps, and a book-case with thirty or forty books in it.

When Silindu entered the room with the Ratemahatmaya, the magistrate was lying in a long chair reading a book. He got up and went over to sit down at the writing-table. He was the white Hamadoru, whom Silindu had seen before in the court. He was dressed now in black, in evening-dress. He sat back in his chair and stared at Silindu in silence for a minute or two with his 'cat's eyes'; he looked cross and tired. Silindu had instinctively squat-ted down again. The Ratemahatmaya angrily told him to stand up. The magistrate seemed to be lost in thought: he continued to stare at Silindu, and as he did so the look of irritation faded from his face. He noted the hopelessness and suffering in Silindu's face, the slow weariness of effort with which he moved his limbs. 'He need not stand,' he said to the Ratemahatmaya. 'He looks damned tired, poor devil. You can take a chair yourself, Ratemahatmaya. God! This is a nice time to bring me work, and you seem to've brought me a miserable-looking wretch. You say it's a murder case?'

'Yes, sir. Or rather it appears so. I do not know much about it. In fact, sir, only what this man has told me. He appeared at my place just now – not half an hour ago – and says that he has killed the Arachchi of his village and another man. I brought him straight to you, sir.'

'Oh, damn it! That means I'll have to go out there to-morrow. How far is it? Beddagama? I don't know the place.'

'It's up the north track, in the jungle, sir. It must be between fifty or sixty miles away, sir.

'Oh, damn! And there are any number of cases fixed for to-morrow. Well – poor devil – he looks pretty done himself! By Jove! I believe he is the man who was before me as an accused in that theft case the other day. I would not charge him, I remem- ber – no evidence against him. It might have been better for him, perhaps, if I had, and convicted him, too.' He turned to Silindu, and said in Sinhalese, 'You were accused of theft before me a few days ago, weren't you?'

'Yes, Hamadoru.'

'Ah, I thought so. Well, Ratemahatmaya, I suppose I had better record your statement first in form. Come on, now.'

The Ratemahatmaya made a short statement of how Silindu had come to him, and what he had said. The magistrate wrote it down, and then turned to Silindu, and explained to him that the offence with which he was charged was murder, and that he was prepared to take down anything he wished to say, and that anything which he did say would be read out at his trial.

Silindu did not quite understand, but he felt vaguely encour- aged by the white Hamadoru. He had spoken Sinhalese to him; he had not spoken in an angry voice, and he was the same Hamadoru who had told him to clear out of the court when he was charged before.

'It is as the Dissamahatmaya[1] said. I have killed the Arachchi and the Mudalali. If the Hamadoru sends to the village, he will find that what I say is true. The Hamadoru remembers the previous case; he knew that they brought a false case against me.

[1] A term commonly used by villagers, referring to the Ratemahatmaya.

He told me to clear out. But the whole case was false – against Babun, too. Am I to tell everything? I am very tired, Hamadoru. For three days now I have been walking and no food but the jungle fruit and leaves. If I might rest now a little, and sleep until to-morrow ... What can I do? I have told all. I am almost an old man, very poor. What can I do?'

'I think I had better take down what you have to say now. But you need not stand. You had better begin from the case. What happened after that?'

'Aiyo, Hamadoru, aiyo! I am very tired. After the case—— It was a false case. The Arachchi for long had been trying to do me harm. How long I cannot remember, but for many years it seems to me. At that time it was because of my daughter; he wanted to take her from Babun and give her to the Mudalali. Well, after the case I set out for the village with the daughter. And all the way I was thinking – thinking how to end this evil. For I knew well that when they came back to the village it would begin again, all over again. They had put Babun in jail – it was a false case, but how should the Hamadoru know that? – with all the lies they told. And they would get Punchi Menika for the Mudalali. Then, as I went, I thought of the old buffalo who is wounded and charges upon——' Silindu caught sight of the gun and rifle, and stopped. 'Ah! the Hamadoru is a hunter, too? He knows the jungle?' he asked eagerly.

'Yes, I know the jungle.'

'Good; then the Hamadoru will understand. The evil and the killing there—— "Yes, it is time," I thought, "to end the evil. I must kill them both." I was a quiet man in the village, all know that. I harmed no one; I wanted to live quietly. I went back to my compound, and sat down and waited. In the evening came the Punchi Arachchi to his house; I saw him go in. Then I took my gun, and went to him, and said: "Ralahami, you may give the woman to the Mudalali, and in return give me back my chena." The Arachchi thought to himself: "Here is a fool." But he said: "Very well, I will give the chena back to you." Then we started for the chena, and as we went on the track I shot him from behind. He is lying dead there now – on the track which leads from the village to the chena. If the Hamadoru sends some one, he can find the body.'

'Yes, and then?'

'Then, Hamadoru, I loaded the gun again, and went back to the village. There was still the Mudalali. I saw him in the Arachchi's garden. He called to me. "Where is the Arachchi?" I went close up to him – he was standing by the stile, and through it I saw his big belly. I shot him too. He must be dead now.'

'Yes, and then?'

'Then? I went to my house, for the women ran out screaming. I put the gun in my house, and went out into the jungle. I was tired. I am a poor man, and I have harmed no one in the village. I am getting old: I wanted to live quietly in my hut. I wanted to rest, Hamadoru. What good, I thought, to fly into the jungle? Only more evil. So I came straight to the Dissamahatmaya. I told him what I had done. That is all.'

The magistrate wrote down what Silindu said, and when he had finished, sat thinking, the pen in his hand, and looking at Silindu. It was very quiet in the room; outside was heard only the drowsy murmur of the sea. Suddenly the quiet was broken by the heavy breathing and snoring of Silindu, who had fallen asleep where he squatted.

'Leave him alone for a bit,' the magistrate said to the Ratemahatmaya. 'There's nothing more to be got from him to-night. We shall have to push on to Beddagama early to-morrow. I suppose it's true what he says.'

'I think so, sir.'

'Damned curious. I thought he wasn't right in the head when I saw him in court before. Well, I'm glad *I* shan't have to hang him.'

'You think he will be hanged, sir?'

'He'll be sentenced at any rate. Premeditation, on his own showing – clearly. And a good enough motive for murder. A very simple case – so they'll think it. You think so, too?'

'It seems to be a simple case, sir.'

'I see you would make a very good judge, Ratemahatmaya. I don't mind telling you – unofficially of course – that I'm a very bad one. It does not seem at all a simple case to me. *I* shouldn't like to hang Silindu of Beddagama for killing your rascally headman. Now then, Ratemahatmaya, here you are; a Sinhalese gentleman; lived your whole life here, among these people. Let's have your opinion of that chap there. He's a human being, isn't he? What sort of a man is he? And how did he come suddenly to murder two people?'

'It's difficult, sir, for me to understand them; about as difficult as for you, sir. They are very different from us. They are very ignorant. They become angry suddenly, and then, they kill like – like – animals, like the leopard, sir.'

'Savages, you mean. Well, I don't know. I rather doubt it. You don't help the psychologist much, Ratemahatmaya. This man, now: I expect he's a quiet sort of man. All he wanted was to be left alone, poor devil. You don't shoot, I believe, Ratemahat-maya, so you don't know the jungle properly. But it's really the same with the other jungle animals, even your leopard, you know. They just want to be left alone, to sleep quietly in the day, and to get their food quietly at night. They won't touch you if you leave them alone. But if you worry 'em enough; follow 'em up and pen 'em up in a corner or a cave, and shoot ·450 bullets at them out of an express rifle; well, if a bullet doesn't find the lungs or heart or brain, they get angry as you call it, and go out to kill. I don't blame them either. Isn't that true?'

'I believe it is, sir.'

'And it's the same with these jungle people. They want to be left alone, to reap their miserable chenas and eat their miserable kurakkan, to live quietly, as he said, in their miserable huts. I don't think that you know, any more than I do, Ratemahat-maya, what goes on up there in the jungle. He was quiet man in the village, I believe that. He only wanted to be left alone. It must take a lot of cornering and torturing and shooting to rouse a man like that. I expect, as he said, they went on at him for years. This not letting one another alone, it's at the bottom of nine-tenths of the crime and trouble; and in nine-tenths of that nine-tenths there's one of your headmen concerned – whom you are supposed to look after.'

'It's very difficult, sir. They live far away in these little villages.

Many of them are good men and help the villagers. But they are ignorant, too.'

'Oh, I'm not blaming you, Ratemahatmaya. I'm not blaming any one. And it's late if we are to start early to-morrow. You had better take your friend away with you and put him in the lock-up. Tell them to give him some food if he wants it. Good-night.'

The Ratemahatmaya shook Silindu until he woke up. It was some little while before he realised where he was, and then that he had to set out again with the Ratemahatmaya. He turned to the magistrate.

'Where are they taking me to, Hamadoru?'

'You will be taken to the prison. You will have to stay there until you are tried.'

'But I have told the truth to the Hamadoru. Let him give his decision. It is to end it all that I came here.'

'I can't try you. You will have to be tried by the great judge.'

'Aiyo, it is you I wish to judge me. You are a hunter, and know the jungle. If they take me away now, how do I know what will happen? What will they do to me? Let it end now, Hamadoru.'

'I am sorry, but I can't do anything. You will be charged with murder. I can't try you for that. The great judge tries those cases. But no harm will come to you. You will be able to rest in the jail until the trial.'

'And what will they do to me? Will they hang me?'

'I'm afraid I can't tell you even that. You must go with the Dissamahatmaya now.'

Silindu, passive again, followed the Ratemahatmaya out of the room. The latter, grumbling at the late hour and the foolish talk of the magistrate, got into his hackery, and the procession trailed off again into the darkness towards the lock-up. Here a long delay occurred. A sleepy sergeant of police had to be woken up, and the whole story had to be explained to him. Eventually Silindu was led away by him and locked up in a narrow bare cell, which, with its immense door made of massive iron bars, was exactly like a cage for some wild animal. In it at last he found himself allowed to lie down and sleep undisturbed.

The rest, which the magistrate had promised him, seemed

however to be still far off; for early next morning he was taken out of his cell and made to start off with the police sergeant for Beddagama. The magistrate, riding on a horse, and the Rate-mahatmaya, in his hackery,[1] passed them when they were two or three miles from the town. A little while afterwards a messenger from Beddagama met the party, bringing the news of the murder to the Ratemahatmaya.

Silindu was being taken to Beddagama to be present at the magistrate's inquiry, but he did not understand this. He was weak and tired after the excitement of the trial and the murder, the long days upon the road, and the little food. He began to think that he had been a fool to give himself up; as he walked behind the police sergeant through the jungle, of which he knew every tree and track, a great desire for it and for freedom came upon him again. He thought of the great bars of the cell door through which he had seen the daylight for the first time that morning. Babun was even now lying behind such bars, and would lie there for six months. And he himself? He might never see the daylight except through such bars now for the rest of his life – unless they hanged him. He thought of the great river that cut through the jungle many miles away: it was pleasant there, to bathe in the cool clear water, and to lie on the bank under the great wild fig-trees in the heat of the day. If he had not given himself up, he might have been there by now, watching the elephant sluicing water over its grey sides or the herd of deer coming down the opposite bank to drink. The thought came to him even now to slip into the jungle and disappear; the fool of a police sergeant would never catch him, would go on for a mile or two probably without knowing that his prisoner had escaped. But he still followed the police sergeant and had not the will or the energy for so decisive a step, for breaking away from the circumstances to which he had always yielded, for taking his life in his hands and moulding it for himself. He had tried once to fight against life when he killed the Arachchi and the Mudalali; he was now caught again in the stream; evil might come, but he could struggle no more.

[1] A hackery is a single bullock-cart.

He had forgotten Punchi Menika until he was a mile or two from the village, and he saw her waiting for him by the side of the track. The rumour had reached the village that Silindu was being brought back by the police in chains. Some said that he was going to be hanged there and then in the village. Punchi Menika had started off to meet him. Her first terror when she had been told of what her father had done had given place to bewilderment, but when she saw him in charge of the police sergeant she ran to him with a cry:

'Is it true, Appochchi; is it true, what they say?'

'What do they say? That I killed those two? It is true I killed them. Then I went to Kamburupitiya and told it all to the Dissamahatmaya and the magistrate Hamadoru.'

'Aiyo, and will they hang you now?'

'What? Do they say that?'

'They say that in the village. It isn't true, is it, Appochchi?'

'I don't know; perhaps it is true, perhaps it isn't. But the magistrate Hamadoru said I would be tried by the great judge.'

'Aiyo! you were mad, Appochchi. It would have been better to have given me to the Mudalali.'

'Hold your tongue, hold your tongue!' burst out Silindu angrily, but his anger died down as rapidly as it had sprung up. 'Don't say that, child, don't say that. No, that is not true, is it, daughter? It is not true. It was for you I did it; and now — after all that — surely in a little all will be well for you.'

'Well? What is to become of me? What am I to do? They will take you away again and hang you, or keep you in the great house over there. And my man, aiyo, is there too. I shall be alone here. What am I to do, Appochchi?'

'Hush! All will be well with you, I tell you. There is no one here to trouble you now. There will be quiet for you again — and for me, perhaps, why not? The killing was for that. Surely, surely, it must be, child. And Babun? Why, in a little while Babun will come back — in a month or two; you will wait in the village, you will sit in the house, in the compound, under the little mustard-tree — so quietly, and the quiet of the great trees, child, round about — nothing to trouble you now. And in a month or two he will come back; he is a good man, Babun, and there will be no evil then – now that the Arachchi is dead and the Mudalali. There will be quiet for you then, and rest.'

'How can I live here alone? There is no food in the house even now.'

'Are not there others in the village? They will help you for a month or two, and they know Babun. He will work hard in the chena and repay them.'

'And you? What will they do to you? Aiyo, aiyo!'

'What does it matter? What have I ever done for you? It was true when they said that I was a useless man in the village. To creep through the leaves like a jackal; yes, I can do that; but what else? Isn't the bad crop in the chena rightly called Silindu's crop. There was never food in my house. The horoscope was true – nothing but trouble and evil and wandering in the jungle. It is a good thing for you that I leave the compound; when I go, good fortune may come.'

'Do not say that, Appochchi; do not say that! To whom did we run in the compound, Hinnihami and I? What father was like you in the village? Must I forget all that now, and sit alone in another's compound begging a little kunji and a handful of kurakkan? No, no! I cannot stay here. Won't they take me away with you to the jail? I cannot live here alone – without you!'

The sergeant looked back and angrily told Punchi Menika to stop making such a noise. They were nearing the village.

'Hush, child,' said Silindu. 'You must stay here. They will not take you, and what could you do in the big town there? You must wait here for Babun.'

The inquiry began as soon as they reached the village. Silindu went with the magistrate, the Ratemahatmaya, the Korala (who had been sent for), and most of the men of the village to the place where the Arachchi had been shot. The body lay where it had fallen; a rough canopy of boughs and leaves had been raised over it to shade it from the sun. A watcher sat near to keep off the pigs and jackals. When the canopy was removed for the magistrate to inspect the body, a swarm of flies rose and hung buzzing in the air above the corpse. The body had not been moved; it lay on its face, the legs half drawn up under the stomach. The blood had dried in great black clots over the wounds on the back. The magistrate looked at it, and then the Korala turned it over. A glaze of grey film was over the eyes. The hot air in the jungle track was heavy with the smell of putrefaction. The crowd of villagers, interested but unmoved, stood watching in the background, while the magistrate, sitting on the stump of a tree, began to write, noting down the position and condition in which he had found the body. Then the doctor arrived and began to cut up the body, where it lay, for post-mortem examination.

The magistrate walked back slowly to the village, followed by Silindu and the headman and such of the spectators as were more interested in the inquiry than in the post-mortem. The same procedure of inspection was gone through with Fernando's body, which lay under another little canopy, where he had died by the stile of the Arachchi's compound. After the inspection came the inquiry: a table and chair had been placed under a large tamarind-tree for the magistrate to write at. The witnesses were brought up, examined, and their statements written down. After each had made his statement, Silindu was told that he could ask them any questions which he wanted them to answer. He had none. The afternoon dragged on; there was no wind, but the heat seemed to come in waves across the village, bringing with it the faint smell of decaying human flesh. The dreary procession of witnesses, listless and perspiring, continued to pass before the tired irritable magistrate. One told how he had seen Silindu and the Arachchi leave the village, Silindu walking behind and carrying a gun; another had heard a shot from the direction of the chena; another had seen Silindu return by himself to the village carrying a gun. The Arachchi's wife told of Silindu's early visit to the hut, of how he left with the Arachchi, of how later, hearing the report of a gun followed by screams, she ran out of the house to see Silindu standing with a smoking gun in his hand and Fernando writhing on the ground near the stile.

Late in the afternoon the inquiry was over. As the Ratemahat-maya had said, it was a simple case. Silindu was remanded, and would certainly be tried for murder before a Supreme Court judge. For the present he was handed over to the police sergeant, with whom he slept that night in a hut in the village. Next day he was taken back to Kamburupitiya, where he again spent the night in the lock-up. Then he was handed over to a fiscal's peon, who put handcuffs on him and started with him along the dusty main road which ran towards the west. They walked slowly along the road for two days. The peon was a talkative man, and he tried to make Silindu talk with him, but he soon gave up the attempt. He had to fall back for conversation on any chance traveller going the same way towards Tangalla where the prison was.

'This fellow,' he would explain to them, pointing to Silindu, 'has killed two men. He will be hanged, certainly he will be hanged. But he's mad. Not a word can you get out of him. He walks along like that mile after mile, looking from side to side – never a word. He thinks there are elephants on the main road I suppose. He comes from up there – in the jungle. They are all cattle like that there of course. I would rather drive a bull along the road than him.'

They passed through several villages, where Silindu was an object of great interest. People came out of the houses and boutiques, and discussed him and his crimes with the peon. The first night they slept in a boutique in one of these villages. The boutique was full of people; they gathered round to watch Silindu eat his curry and rice with his handcuffed hands. They too discussed him in loud tones with the peon. There were two traders on their way to Kamburupitiya; the rest, with the exception of one old man, belonged to the village. This old man was one of those wanderers whom one meets from time to time in villages, upon the roads, or even sometimes in the jungle. Very old, very dirty, with long matted hair and wild eyes, he sat mumbling to himself in a corner. A beggar and mad, he had two claims to the charity of the boutique-keeper, who had taken him in for the night and given him a good meal of curry and rice.

The peon had for the twentieth time that day told Silindu's story with many embellishments, and complained bitterly of his silence and stupidity. The others sat round in the reeking atmosphere watching Silindu eat his rice by the dim light of two oil wicks.

'Will they hang him, aiya?' asked the boutique-keeper.

'Yes, he'll be hanged, sure enough,' said the peon. 'He confessed it himself, you see.'

'But they never really hang people, I am told. They send them away to a prison a long way off. They say they hang them just to frighten people.'

The other villagers murmured approval. The peon laughed.

'Of course they hang them. I've known people who were hanged. Why Balappu, who lived next door to me in Kamburu-pitiya, was hanged. He quarrelled with his brother in the street outside my house – it was about a share in their land – and he stabbed him dead. They hanged him. I took him along this same road to the prison three years ago. A good man he was: wanted to gamble all along the road.'

'But you don't know that he was hanged, aiya. No one saw it, no one ever sees it.'

'Nonsense,' said one of the traders. 'In Maha Nuwara they hang them. I knew a man there whose nephew was hanged, and afterwards they gave him the body to bury. The head hung over like this, and the mark of the rope was round the neck.'

The old beggar had listened to what was going on, squatting in his corner. He did not get up, but shuffled slowly forward into the circle, still in a squatting position. Silindu, who had before shown little interest in the conversation, looked up when the beggar intervened.

'Aiyo! what's that you say?' the old man asked. 'They are going to hang this man? Why's that?'

'He shot two men dead up there in the jungle.'

'Chi! chi! why did he do that?'

'He's mad, father, as mad as you.'

The old man turned and looked hard at Silindu, while Silindu stared at him. The spectators laughed at the curious sight. The old man smiled.

'He's not mad,' he said. 'Not as mad as I am. So he killed twice, did he? Dear, dear. The Lord Buddha said: Kill not at all, kill nothing. It is a sin to kill. If he saw a caterpillar in the path, he put his foot on one side. Man, man why have you killed twice? Were you mad?'

'I'm not mad,' said Silindu. 'They were hunting me: they would have killed me. Therefore I killed them.'

'The man is not mad, no more mad than you, or you – but I – I am mad. So at least they say. Why do they say that I'm mad? My son, do you see this paper?' (He showed a very dirty English newspaper to Silindu.) 'Well, if you are quite quiet and no gecko[1] cries and the jackals don't howl, I will look at it like this afterwards, for some short time – staring hard – then I shall see things on the paper, not the writing – I have wandered all my life – a wanderer on the path, seeking merit by the Three Gems – I cannot read writing or letters – but I shall see things themselves, a little hut up there in the jungle, if you desire it – your hut, my son – and I'll tell you what is doing there, that the woman is lying in the hut, crying perhaps. This paper was given to me by a white Mahatmaya whom I met out there once, also in the jungle. It is of great power: before I could only see what was doing in this country; but now, by its help, I can see over the sea, to the white Mahatmaya's country. Then they say: this is a mad old man. Well, well, who knows? I am always on the path – to-morrow I shall leave this village – from village to village, from town to town, and from jungle to jungle. I see many different men on the path. Strange men, and they do strange things. Thieving, stabbing, killing, cultivating paddy. I do not cultivate paddy, nor do I thieve or kill. I am mad perhaps. But very often it is they who seem to me to want but a little to be mad. All this doing and doing, – running round and round like the red ants – thieving, stabbing, killing, cultivating this and that. Is there much good or wisdom in such a life? It seems to me full of evil – nothing but evil and trouble. Do they ever sit down and rest, do they ever meditate? Desire and desire again, and no fulfilment ever. Is such a life sane or mad? Did they call you mad in the village even before this, my son?'

[1] The common lizard: its 'chirp' is always considered by the Sinhalese to be a warning or sign of ill omen.

'Yes, the mad hunter,' said Silindu, and the others laughed again.

'Ah, you are a hunter too. That also I have not done. But I know the jungle, for I travel through it often on my path. Do the beasts in it speak to you, son hunter?'

'Yes. They used to speak to me.'

'So they called you mad. All the beasts in the jungle speak to me too, except the elephant. The elephant is too sad even to talk. Usually when I see him he is eating; for he is always hungry because of his sins in the previous birth. But sometimes I find him standing alone away among the rocks, swaying from side to side. He is very sad, thinking of his sins in the previous birth. Then I say to him, "Brother, your feet too are upon the path. It is good to think of the sins of the previous birth, but there is no need of such sadness." Then he sways more and more, and his trunk moves from side to side, and he lifts one foot up after the other very slowly, but he never says a word, watching me with his little eye. Once, indeed, I remember, he lifted up his trunk and screamed. I too lifted up my hands and cried out with him, for we were both on the path.'

'You do not know the jungle, father,' said Silindu. 'It is of food and killing and hunting that the beasts talk to me. They know nothing of your path, nor do I.'

'Aiyo, it is not only in the jungle that they say that. They say the same in the small villages and the great towns. What do you say, sir?' he said, turning to one of the traders.

'I do not go into the jungle or talk to elephants, old man,' said the trader. 'I know the bazaar, and there they think of fanams[1] first and the path last.'

'A man must live,' said the other trader. 'It is only priests and beggars who have full bellies and idle hands.'

'The Lord Buddha was a beggar and a priest too,' said the old man, and began to mumble to himself. The laugh was against the trader.

'Aiya,' said the old man to the peon, 'who is going to hang this hunter?'

---

[1] Pence.

'The Government of course. He will be tried by the judge, and then they will hang him.'

'This is another thing which I do not understand. To the madman this seems foolish to kill a man because he has killed. If it is a sin, will he not be punished in the next birth?'

The old beggar had a strange influence on Silindu, who watched him the whole time, fascinated. The mumbled words seemed to excite him greatly.

'What do you mean, father?' he said, his voice rising. 'How punished in the next birth? They will punish me here – the judge – they do that – they will hang me – you hear what these have said.'

'I do not know about that. I only know of the path. On my way through the villages I hear them say this or that, but I do not understand. To-morrow I shall be gone, to the east, and you to the west. Do you know, my son, where you will sleep to-morrow night? No, no. Nor I either. But we go on the path each of us, because of the sins in our previous births. As the Lord Buddha said to the she-devil, "O fool! fool! Because of your sins in the former birth, you have been born a she-devil: and yet you go on committing sins even now. What folly!" Is not that clear? Of these punishments of the Government I know nothing. If they are punishments they are because of sins committed in your previous birth; but be sure that for the sins which you commit in this birth – for the killing – for that is a sin, a great sin – you will be punished in the next birth. How many will hell await there! Surely, son, it is better to wander on and on from village to village, always, begging a little rice and avoiding sin.'

'But surely I have committed no sin. All these years they plagued me, and did evil to me. Was I to be starved by them, and my daughter starved? Was I to allow them to take her from me and from Babun?'

'The Lord Buddha said, "It is a sin to kill, even the louse in the hair must not be cracked between the nails." The other things I do not understand. I have no daughter and no wife and no hut. It is better to be without. They stand in one's way on the path. And to starve? What need to starve, my son? In every village is a handful of rice for the wanderer. As for the hanging, that is very foolish; the judge must be a foolish man, but I do not think it will hurt you. Remember it is not for the killing of the two men, but for the previous birth. Then there comes hell. You must have killed many deer and pig.'

'Yes, yes, I am a hunter, but what of that, father, what of that?'

'Each is a sin, for I told you, didn't I, that the Lord Buddha said, "It is a sin to kill." My son, you are a hunter, you know the jungle; surely you have seen the evil there, and the pain – always desire and killing. No peace or rest there either for the deer or the pig, or the little grey mongoose. They have sinned, and are far from Nirvana and happiness; and, like the she-devil, they sin again only to bring more evil on themselves by their blindness. What happiness is there in it, my son? The deer and the pig, they too are upon the path. It was greater sin to kill them than the other two. For those two, you say, were bringing evil upon you; but what did the deer and pig do to you? eh, hunter? tell me that.'

'Do? Nothing, of course. But there is no food up there. One must have food to live.'

'No food up there? There is always food upon the path, a handful of rice in every village, for the beggar. I have been forty years now on the path. Have I starved?'

'What was your village, father?'

'The name – I have forgotten – but it lay up there in the hills – a pleasant place – rain in plenty, and the little streams always running into the rice-fields, and cocoa-nut and areca-nut trees all around.'

'Ohé!' murmured one of the villagers, 'it is easy to avoid killing in a place like that.'

'Have you ever worked, old man?' said the peon. 'Have you ever earned a fanam by work? In this part of the country rupees don't grow on wara[1] bushes.'

'No,' said the old man; 'I have never done anything like that. I am mad, you know. I remember once they took me to the field to

[1] A shrub which grows in waste places.

watch — I was a boy — I had to scare the birds away. I was there alone, sitting under a small tree beside the field. The little birds came in crowds to feed on the young paddy. They were very hungry. What harm, I thought, if they eat a little? Plenty will remain for the house. So I sat there thinking of other things, and I forgot about the paddy and the birds until my father came and beat me. After that they took me no more to the fields; and I sat in the compound all day, thinking foolish things, until at last an old priest came by, and he told me of the path, and how to meditate, and I followed him. He died many years ago, many years. I have been no more to my village, it is forgotten; but I think it was up there in the hills; it is very long ago, and I have seen many villages since then. They are all the same; even the names I never know; always some huts, and men and women and children, suffering punishment for their sins and sinning again.'

'This is fool's talk,' said the peon impatiently. 'We cannot all beg upon the road. I have heard the priests themselves say that every one cannot reach Nirvana. Nor are we all mad. There are the women and the children. Are they too to become holy men? It is hard enough to live on the eleven rupees which the Government gives us. I don't kill deer, but I eat it when I can get it. Is that too a sin, old man?'

But before the old beggar could answer, Silindu threw himself down on the ground in front of him, and touching his feet with his hands burst out:

'It is true, father, it is true what you say. I did not understand before, though I knew; yes, I knew it well. I have seen it all so long in the jungle. But I did not understand. How many times have I told the little ones — not understanding — about it all. Always this killing, killing, killing; everything afraid: the deer and the pig and the jackal after them, and the leopard himself. Always evil there. No peace, no rest — it was rest I wanted. It is true, father, I have seen it, it is the punishment for their sins. And always evil for me too, there; hunger always and trouble always. You should have shown me this path of yours before, father; even now I do not understand that, and it would be useless now.

Through all the evil I have but sinned more, killing the deer and the pig, and now these two men. It is too late. They will hang me, they will hang me, and what then, old man, what then?'

The old man began to shake with laughter. He mumbled incoherently, pulling at his beard and long hair with his hands. The scene caused great pleasure and amusement to all the others, except the peon, who was annoyed at finding that he was no longer playing the most important part. After a while the old man's laughter began to subside, and he regained sufficient control to make himself intelligible.

'Well, well,' he said, 'well, well, I'm not the Lord Buddha, my son. Well, well. D'you see that? He touches my feet as though I were the Lord Buddha himself. I have never seen that before, and I have seen many strange things. I am become a holy man; well, well.' Here again he was overcome with silent laughter.

'Do not laugh, father,' said Silindu. 'Why do you laugh? Is it lies that you told me just now?'

The other became serious again at once.

'Lies? No, no. I do not tell lies. Aiyo, it is all true. But what was it you were saying just then? Ah, yes. You were afraid, afraid of the hanging and the punishment, and of the next birth. Too late, you said, too late for the path. My son, it is never too late to acquire merit. Perhaps they will hang you, perhaps not. Who can say? It matters little, for it will be as it will be. I do not think it will hurt very much. And before that, it is possible for you to acquire much merit. It will help you much in the next birth. You must meditate: you must think of holy things. Here are holy words for you to learn.' He repeated a Pali stanza, and tried to make Silindu learn it. It was a difficult task, and it was only after innumerable repetitions that Silindu at last got it by heart. When he had at last done so, he sat mumbling it over to himself again and again, so as not to forget it.

'That is good,' went on the old man. 'Along the road as you go – wherever you are going – to the prison or to the hanging – repeat the holy words many times. In that way you will acquire merit. Also meditate on your sins, the sin of killing, the deer and pig which you have killed. So you will acquire merit too. And avoid killing. Remember, if there were a caterpillar in the path, he put his foot on one side. So too you will acquire merit. It will help you in the next birth. I think you are already on the path, my son. And perhaps if my path too leads me to the west, who knows? I shall see you there again, and we shall talk together. Now, however, I grow tired.'

So saying the old man shuffled back into a corner, and covering his head and face with a dirty cloth, soon fell asleep. Silindu continued to mumble the Pali stanza, which he did not understand. The villagers, seeing that no more amusement was to be obtained from the strangers, left the boutique; and the boutique-keeper and the other travellers soon after spread out their mats on the ground, and lay down to sleep.

The next day the peon and Silindu started off very early in the morning. All along the road Silindu repeated the holy words to the great annoyance of the peon. They reached the prison at Tangalla late in the evening. It was dark when they arrived, and Silindu was at once locked up in a cell. He fell asleep, still repeating the Pali stanza.

Silindu remained three weeks in the prison. It seemed to him an immense building. It was a large and ancient Dutch fort, with high battlemented grey walls of great thickness. The inside formed a square paved courtyard in which the prisoners worked at breaking stones and preparing coir[1] by hammering cocoa-nut husks with wooden mallets. Round the courtyard were built the cells, oblong bare rooms with immense windows and gates, iron barred, which looked out upon the yard. Silindu, not being a convicted person, was not made to do any work. He squatted in his cell, watching the prisoners working in the yard, and thinking of what the old beggar had told him. He tried to meditate upon his sins, but soon found that to be impossible. He began, however, to forget the village and Punchi Menika, and all the trouble that had gone before. He repeated the Pali stanza many times during the day. He was very happy; he grew fat upon the good prison food.

[1] Coir, fibre of the cocoa-nut husk.

Only once was the monotony of the days broken for him. He was watching a group of prisoners, in their blue and white striped prison clothes; they all looked almost exactly alike. They were quite near the gate of his cell, filling the bathing-trough with water. Suddenly in one of them he recognized Babun. He jumped up and ran to the bars of the gate, crying out:

'Ohé! Babun! Babun!'

Babun looked round. There was no surprise or interest in his face, when he saw that it was Silindu. A great change had come over him in the short time during which he had been in prison. His skin, a sickly yellow colour, seemed to have shrunk with the flesh and muscle, which had wasted; he was bent and stooping; his eyes were sunken; a look of dullness and hopelessness was in his face. He looked at Silindu frowning. Silindu danced about with excitement behind the bars.

'You know me, Babun?' he shouted. 'You know me? Why do you look like that? All is well, all is well. I shot the Arachchi and Fernando: they are dead. But all is well. They'll hang me. That's why I'm here. But I have my feet on the path. I've acquired merit. The old man was right.'

A jail guard shouted across the courtyard to Silindo to 'shut his mouth.'

'And the woman,' said Babun, in a low, dull voice. 'Where is the woman?'

'She is there in the village waiting for you. All is well, I tell you. They are dead: I killed them. It was the only way, though a sin, a great sin, the old man said. They will hang me, every one says so; but all is well, I've found the path. And you – you'll go back to the village. Punchi Menika is there, waiting. The evil is over.'

Babun stared at him, frowning. His face had lost completely the open cheerful look which it had once had. At last he said slowly:

'You are mad. I don't understand you. If you have killed those two, you are a fool, madman. What's the good? I shall never go back there. I shall die here. And you? Yes, they'll hang you, as you say. What's the good? You are mad, mad – you always were.'

He turned away, and slowly lifting the pail of water emptied it into the trough.

Silindu often saw Babun again in the yard, but never spoke to him. Babun seemed purposely to avoid passing near his cell, and if he had to do so, he kept his eyes fixed on the ground. The day of Silindu's trial arrived. In the morning he was taken out of his cell, and handed over with four other prisoners to an escort of police. They put handcuffs on his hands, and led him through the streets to the court.

Silindu's case was the first case for trial. He did not pay much attention to the proceedings – he continued to mumble the Pali stanza – but he felt the greater pomp and solemnity of this court compared with the police court. The judge was a grey-haired man in a dull scarlet gown. There was a jury, among which were several white Mahatmayas; there were a great many lawyers sitting round the table in the centre of the court; and there was a crowd of officials and policemen standing about.

Silindu had an advocate assigned to him by the court to defend him. The lawyer soon found it useless to discuss the case with the prisoner: the line of defence was clear, however; he would admit the killing, and plead insanity and provocation. The indictment for murder was read, and the witnesses for the prosecution then gave their evidence. They were cross-examined by Silindu's advocate, only with a view to showing that it had been well known in the village that Silindu was mad: they admitted that he had always been 'tikak pissu.' They none of them knew anything about a quarrel with the Arachchi before the theft and the conviction of Babun.

Silindu's advocate then put him in the witness-box. He repeated the statement which he had made to the magistrate. He was asked very few questions in cross-examination, but the judge examined him at some length. The judge's object was to make it clear, when the idea of killing the two men first came to Silindu, and what was in Silindu's mind during his walk to the chena with the Arachchi. Silindu understood nothing of what

was going on; he did not know, and could not have been made
to understand the law; he understood the point and reason for
no single question asked him. He knew he would be hanged; he
was tired of this continual slow torture of questions which he
had to answer; he wanted only to be left in peace to repeat the
holy words again and again: he had told them of the killing so
many times; why should they continue to bother him with these
perpetual questions? He answered the questions indifferently,
badly. Most of those in the court listening to his bare passionless
sentences describing how he determined to kill the two men,
how he watched for their return to the village, sitting all day long
in his compound, and how he finally killed them on the next day,
were left with the conviction that they had before them a brutal
and cold murderer.

The summing up of the judge, however, showed that he was
not one of those who regarded it as a simple case. He laid stress
on the fact that the prisoner had never been considered in the
village to be completely sane, and he directed the notice of the
jury to the 'queer' ideas which the prisoner seemed to have had
in his mind about the hunting and his own identification with the
buffalo. It was right for them also to consider the demeanour of
the prisoner while in court, his apparent listlessness and lack of
interest in what was going on. They must, however, remember
that if the defence of insanity was to succeed, they must be
satisfied that the prisoner was actually incapable, owing to
unsoundness of mind, of knowing the nature of his act, or of
knowing that he was doing what was wrong or contrary to law.

After the judge had summed up, the jury were told they could
retire to consider their verdict, but after consulting with them,
the foreman stated they were all agreed that the prisoner was
guilty of murder. Silindu was still muttering his stanza; he had
not tried to understand what was going on around him. The court
interpreter went close up to the dock and told him that the jury
had found him guilty of murder. Was there anything which he
had to say why sentence of death should not be passed on him?
A curious stillness had fallen on the place. Silindu suddenly
became conscious of where he was: he looked round and saw

that every one was looking at him; he saw the faces of the crowd outside staring through the windows and craning round the pillars on the verandah; all the eyes were staring at him as if something was expected from him. For a moment the new sense of comfort and peace left him; he felt afraid again, hunted; he looked up and down the court as if in search of some path of escape.

'Aiyo!' he said to the interpreter, 'does that mean I am to be hanged?'

'Have you anything to say why you should not be sentenced to be hanged?'

'What is there to say? I have known that a long time. They told me that I should be hanged – all the people – along the road. What is there to say now, aiya?'

Silindu's words were interpreted to the judge, who took up a black cloth and placed it on his head. Silindu was sentenced to be hanged by the neck until he should be dead. The words were translated to him in Sinhalese by the interpreter. He began again to repeat the stanza. He was taken out of the court, handcuffed, and escorted back to his cell in the prison by five policemen armed with rifles.

He was to be hanged in two weeks' time, and the days passed for him peacefully as the days had passed before the trial. He had no fear of the hanging now. If he had any feeling towards it, it was one of expectancy, even hope. Vaguely he looked forward to the day as the end of some long period of evil, as the beginning of something happier and better. He scarcely thought of the actual hanging, but when he did, he thought of it in the words of the old beggar, 'I do not think it will hurt much.'

Four days before the day fixed for the execution, the jailer came to Silindu's cell accompanied by a Sinhalese gentleman dressed very beautifully in European clothes and a light grey sun-helmet. Silindu was told to get up and come forward to the window of the cell. The Sinhalese gentleman then took a document out of his pocket and began reading it aloud in a high pompous voice. It informed Silindu that the sentence of death passed on him had been commuted to one of twenty years' rigorous imprisonment. When the reading stopped, Silindu continued to stare vacantly at the gentleman.

'Do you understand, fellow?' said the latter.

'I don't understand, Hamadoru.'

'Explain to him, jailer.'

'You are not going to be hanged, d'you understand that? You'll be kept in prison instead – twenty years.'

'Twenty years?'

'Yes, twenty years. D'you understand that?'

Silindu did not understand it. He could understand a week or two weeks, or a month, or even six months, but twenty years meant nothing to him. It was just a long time. At any rate he was not, after all, to be hanged. For the moment a slight sense of uneasiness and disappointment came over him. In the last four days he had grown to look forward to the end, and now the end was put off for twenty years, for ever, it seemed to him. He squatted down by the gate of his cell, holding the great iron bars in his hands and staring out into the courtyard. He thought of the past three weeks which he had spent in the cell; after all, they had been very peaceful and happy. He had been acquiring merit, as the old man told him to do. Now he would have more time still for acquiring it. He would be left in peace here for twenty years – for a lifetime – to acquire merit, and at the end he might make his way back to the village and find Babun and Punchi Menika there, and sit in their compound again watching the shadows of the jungle. It was very peaceful in the cell.

A jail guard came and unlocked the cell gate. Silindu was taken out and made to squat down in the long shed which ran down the centre of the courtyard. A wooden mallet was put into his hand and a pile of cocoanut husk thrown down in front of him. For the remainder of that day, and daily for the remainder of twenty years, he had to make coir by beating cocoanut husks with the wooden mallet.

CHAPTER IX

PUNCHI MENIKA had been present at the inquiry of the magistrate in the village, but she had not spoken to Silindu after her meeting with him when he was being brought to Beddagama by the police sergeant. The magistrate and the headman and the prisoner had left for Kamburupitiya very early in the morning following the day of the inquiry. She and the other villagers woke up to find that the village had already been left to its usual sleepy life. There was nothing for her to do but to obey Silindu's instructions, to wait for Babun's release, living as best she might in the hut with Karlinahami. Her present misfortunes, the imprisonment of Babun, the loss of her father, and the fate (and the uncertainty of it) which hung over him, weighed numbly upon her. And the future filled her with vague fears; she did not, could not plan about it, or calculate about it, or visualise it, or anything in it. She did not even think definitely of how she was going to live for six months, until Babun should return. There was scarcely food in the house for her and Karlinahami to exist in semi-starvation through those six months. Yet the future loomed somehow upon her, filling her with a horrible sense of uneasiness, uncertainty. It was a new feeling. She sat in the hut silent and frightened the greater part of the day. She thought of Silindu's stories of hunters who had lost their way in the jungle. Their terror must have been very like hers; she was alone, terribly alone and deserted; she too had lost her way, and like them one path was as good or as bad to her as another.

Karlinahami was nearly fifty years old now, and in a jungle village a woman – and especially a woman without a husband – is very old, very near the grave at fifty. The sun and the wind, the toil, the hunger, and the disease sap the strength of body and mind, bring folds and lines into the skin, and dry up the breasts. A woman is old at forty or even thirty. No one, man or woman, in the jungle, lives to the term of years allotted to man. It would have been difficult to say whether Karlinahami looked nearer eighty than ninety, nearer ninety than a hundred. The jungle had left its mark on her. Her body was bent and twisted, like the stunted trees, which the south-west wind had tortured into grotesque shapes. The skin, too, on her face and thin limbs reminded one of the bark of the jungle trees; it was shrunken against the bones, and wrinkled, and here and there flaking off into whitish brown scales, as the bark flakes off the kumbuk-trees. The flesh of the cheeks had dried and shrunk; the lips seemed to have sunk into the toothless mouth, leaving a long line damp with saliva under the nose. And under the lined forehead were the eyes, lifeless and filmy, peering out of innumerable wrinkles. The eyes were not blind, but they seemed to be sightless – the pupil, the iris, and even the white had merged – because the mind was dying. It is what usually happens in the jungle – to women especially – the mind dies before the body. Imperceptibly the power of initiative, of thought, of feeling, dies out before the monotony of life, the monotony of the tearing hot wind, the monotony of endless trees, the monotony of perpetual hardship. It will happen at an age when in other climates a man is in his prime, and a woman still bears children. The man will still help at the work in the chena, cutting down the under-growth and sowing the crop; but he will do so unthinking, without feeling, like a machine or an animal; and when it is done he will sit hour after hour in his compound staring with his filmy eyes into nothing, motionless, except when he winds one long thin arm round himself, like a grey monkey, and scratches himself on the back. And the woman still carries the waterpot to the muddy pool to fetch water; still cooks the meal in the house. While they still stand upright, they must do their work; they eat and they sleep; they mutter frequently to themselves; but they do not speak to others, and no one speaks to them. They live in a twilight, where even pain is scarcely felt.

Karlinahami was sinking rapidly into this twilight. In the jungle decay and growth are equally swift. The trial of Silindu and Babun, the murder of the Arachchi and Fernando, and now the loss of Silindu had meant very little to her. She had felt vaguely that many evils were happening, but facts no longer had

[…] She fetched the water as usual for
[…se]lf; but she did not speak to Punchi
[…] knew that to talk to her or consult

[…]on of Silindu the life of the village
[…appe]ared to have regained its ordinary
[…] change had come over it. It had
[…]dling village before; one of those
[…]cay, to fade out at last into the
[…]blow, in a day, it lost one out of its
[…it]s twenty-five inhabitants. For after
[…N]anchohami, his wife, decided to
[…] were too young to do chena work;
[…] any longer to support herself in
[…wh]ere the Arachchi's relations lived,
[…pe]anuts, and rain fell in plenty every
[…] hut, and a little land; she would
[…] had always said that Beddagama
[…e]vil and evil omens. She packed up
[…o]ck hackery, which she borrowed
[…]r Kotegoda. The Arachchi's house
[…] There was no one to inhabit it;
[…] been foolhardy enough to go and
[…] cursed, and very soon came to be
[…] It seemed to make a long fight
[…] itself merged into the low scrub
[…] into a thick line of small trees. The
[…]le grey thick leaves and purple
[…]reat spined slabs of prickly pear,
[…] shadow of the fence over the
[…] the very door. But the walls were
[…] those of most huts: the roof was of
[…]tch to be torn and scattered by the
[…] of the north-east monsoon beat
[…]o years in vain; they washed out
[…]hich you could see the jungle sticks

upon which the mud had been plastered. The sticks exposed to the damp air took root and burst into leaf. Great weeds, and even bushes, began to grow up between the tiles, from seeds dropped by birds or scattered by the wind. An immense twisted cactus towered over the roof. The tiles were dislodged and pushed aside by the roots. The jungle was bursting through the walls, overwhelming the house from above. The jungle moved within the walls: at last they crumbled; the tiled roof fell in. The grass and the weeds grew up over the little mound of broken red pottery; the jungle sticks of the walls spread out into thick bushes. Tall saplings of larger trees began to show themselves. By the end of the third rains the compound and the house had been blotted out.

It was as if the jungle had broken into the village. Other huts had been abandoned, overwhelmed, blotted out before, but they had always lain on the outside of the village. The jungle had only drawn its ring closer round the remaining huts; it had not broken into the village – the village had remained a whole, intact. But now the jungle cut across the village, separating Silindu's and Bastian Appu's hut from the rest. The villagers themselves noted it: they felt that they were living in a doomed place. 'The village is dying,' Nanchohami had said before she left. 'An evil place, devil-haunted. It is dying, as its young die with the old. No children are born in it now. An evil place. In ten years it will have gone, trampled by the elephants.'

It was, however, only very gradually that this feeling of doom came to be felt by the village and the villagers. At first, after the excitement of the trials and the murder, they seemed to have settled down to the old monotonous life, as it had been before. The vederala was appointed Arachchi. Punchi Menika waited for Babun. She did not and could not count the passing of time: a week was only some days to her, and six months only many months; but she waited, watching the passage of time, vaguely but continuously, for the day when Babun should return. She head the rumour which eventually reached the village that after all Silindu was not to be hanged; he was to be kept in prison, they said, for ever, for the remainder of his life. It brought no comfort to her; he had been taken out of her life, she would never see him again; did it matter whether he was dead or in prison?

She waited month after month. Her first feelings of fear were lost in the perpetual sense of expectancy as the time slipped away. And she had to work, to labour hard in order to keep herself and Karlinahami alive. The little store of kurakkan in the house dwindled rapidly. She had to search the jungle for edible leaves and wild fruit and roots, like the wild onions which the pig feed upon. When the chena season came she worked in the others' chenas, Balappu's and Bastian Appu's, and even Punchirala's. She worked hard like a man for a few handfuls of kurakkan, given to her as a charity. The others liked her, and were in their way kind to her; they liked her quietness, her gentleness and submission. Even Punchirala said of her: 'She goes about like a doe. They used to call the mad vedda a leopard. The leopard's cub has turned into a deer.'

As the months passed, she gradually began to feel as if each day might be the one on which Babun would return. And as each day passed without bringing him, she tried to reckon whether the six months had really gone. She talked it over with the other villagers. Some said it was five months, others seven months since the conviction. They discussed it for hours, wrangling, quarrelling, shouting at one another. He had been convicted two months – about two months – before the Sinhalese New Year. 'No, it was one month before the New Year.' 'It couldn't be one month before, because the chena crop was not reaped yet.' 'Reaped? Why it had only just been sown.' 'It must have been three months before.' 'Three months, you fool? Is a chena crop like ninety days' rice?' 'Fool? Who is a fool?' 'Hold your tongue! Hold your tongue! At any rate, it was before the New Year, and it's already six months since the New Year.' 'Aiyo! Six months since the New Year. It is only a month since I sowed my chena. Who ever heard of sowing a chena five months after the New Year? It is not three months since the New Year.'

Punchi Menika would stand listening to them going over it again and again, hour after hour. She listened in silence, and would then slip quietly away to wander in the evening down the track towards Kamburupitiya. It was on the track that she hoped, that she was certain that she would meet him. Then all would be well; the evil would end, as Silindu had said. But as the days went by, the certainty left her; even hope began to tremble, to give place to forebodings, fears. The time came when all were agreed that the six months had passed; something must have happened to him; he was ill, perhaps, or he had just been forgotten there; one can never tell, anything may happen when a man gets into prison; 'they' simply have forgotten to let him out.

Punchirala, the new headman, was consulted. 'The man,' he said, 'is probably dead.' Punchi Menika shuddered. Her great eyes, in which the look of suffering had already grown profound and steady, did not leave the vederala's face. 'Yes, I expect the man's dead. They die quickly over there in prison. Especially strong men like Babun. They lie down in a corner and die. There is medicine for diseases, but is there any medicine for fate? So they say, and lie down in the corner and die. There is nothing for you to do. No. I can give you no medicine for fate either. You must sit down here in the village and marry a young man – if you can find one, and if not, perhaps, an old one. Eh? Why not? Though the jackals are picking the bones of the elephant on the river bank, there are other elephants bathing in the river. Nor are they all cows. Well, well.'

'Ralahami, do you really know anything? Have you heard that he is dead?'

'I have heard nothing. From whom could I hear? If you want to hear anything you must go to the prison. It will take you many days – first to Kamburupitiya, and then west along the great road, three days to Tangalla, where the prison is. You must ask at the prison. They can tell you.'

Punchi Menika left the vederala in silence. She walked away very slowly to the hut; the conviction had come to her at once that she must go to the prison. The thought of the journey alone into an unknown world frightened her; but she felt that she must go, that she could not bear any longer this waiting in doubt in the village. She made some cakes of kurakkan, tied them up in a handkerchief, together with some uncooked grain which the villagers gave her when they heard of her intended journey, and started next day for Kamburupitiya.

The first part of her journey, the track to Kamburupitiya, she knew well. She had, too, no fear, as other women have, of being alone in the jungle. It was when she turned west along the main road to Tangalla that her real troubles began. She felt lost and terribly alone on the straight, white, dusty road. The great clumsy bullock carts, laden with salt or paddy, perpetually rumbled by her; the carters she knew were bad men, terrible tales were told about them in the villages. The life of the road frightened her far more than the silence and solitude of the jungle. That she understood: she belonged to it. But the stream of passers-by upon the road, the unknown faces and the eyes that always stared strangely, inquiringly at her for a moment, and had then passed on for ever, made her feel vaguely how utterly alone she was in the world. And nowhere was this feeling so strong for her as in the villages which she slunk through like a frightened jackal. Everywhere it was the same; the crowd of villagers and travellers staring at her from in front of the village boutique, the group of women gossiping and laughing round the well in the paddy field – not a known face among them all. She had not the courage even to ask to be allowed to sleep at night in a boutique or hut. She preferred to creep into some small piece of jungle by the roadside, when darkness found her tired and hungry.

She was very tired and very hungry before she reached Tangalla. Her bewilderment was increased by the network of narrow streets. She wandered about until she suddenly found herself in the market. It was market-day, and a crowd of four or five hundred people were packed together into the narrow space, which was littered with the goods and produce which they were buying and selling: fruit and vegetables and grain and salt and clothes and pots. Every one was talking, shouting, gesticulating at the same time. The noise terrified her, and she fled away. She hurried down another narrow street, and found herself at the foot of a hill which rose from the middle of the town. There were no houses upon its sides, but there was an immense building on the top of it. There was no crowd there, only an old man sitting on the bare hillside watching five lean cows which were trying to find some stray blades of parched brown grass on the stony soil.

She squatted down, happy in the silence and solitude of the place after the noise of the streets and market. Nothing was to be heard except the cough of one of the cows from time to time, and from far off the faint, confused murmur from the market-place. She looked up at the great white building; it was very glaring and dazzling in the blaze of the sun. She wondered whether it was the prison in which Babun lay. She looked at the old man sitting among the five starved cows. He reminded her a little of Silindu; he sat so motionless, staring at a group of cocoanut-trees that lay around the bottom of the hill. He was as thin as the cattle which he watched: as their flanks heaved in the heat you saw the ribs sticking out under their mangy coats, and you could see, too, every bone of his chest and sides panting up and down under his dry, wrinkled skin. The insolent noisy townspeople had frightened her; this withered old man seemed familiar to her, like a friend. He might very easily have come out of the jungle.

She went over to where he sat, and stood in front of him. For a moment he turned on her his eyes, which were covered with a film the colour of the film which forms on stagnant water; then he began again to stare at the palms in silence.

'Father,' she said, 'is that the prison?'

The old man looked up slowly at the great glaring building as if he had seen it for the first time, and then looked from it to Punchi Menika.

'Yes,' he said in a dry husky voice. 'Why?'

'My man must be there,' said Punchi Menika gazing at the white walls. 'He was sent there many months ago. They sent him there for six months. It was a false case. The six months have passed now, but he has not returned to the village. I have come to ask about him here – a long way. I am tired, father, tired of all this. But he must be there.

The old man's eyes remained fixed upon the cocoanut-palms; he did not move.

'What is your village, woman?' he asked.

'I come from Beddagama.'

'Beddagama, I know it. I knew it long ago. I, too, come from over there, from Mahawelagama, beyond Beddagama. You should go back to your village, woman.'

'But my man, father, what about my man?'

The old man turned his head very slowly and looked up at the prison. The sun beat down upon his face, which seemed to have been battered and pinched and folded and lined by age and misery. His eyes wandered from the prison to one of the cows. She stood still, stretching out her head in front of her, her great eyes bulging; she coughed in great spasms which strained her flanks. He waited until the coughing had stopped, and she began again to search the earth for something to eat. Then he said, speaking as if to himself:

'They never come out from there – not if they are from the jungle. How can they live in there, always shut in between walls? These town people – they do not mind, but we—— Surely I should know – I am from Mahawelagama, a village in the jungle over there. I would go back now, but I am too old. When one is old, it is useless; but you—— Go back to your village, woman. It is folly to leave the village. There is hunger there, I know, I remember that; but there is the hut and the compound all by themselves, and the jungle beyond. Here there is nothing but noise and trouble, and one house upon the other.'

'But I must ask at the prison first for my man. Why are they keeping him there?'

'They never come out. Surely I should know. My son was sent there. He never came out. The case was in this town, and I came here and spent all I had for him. Then I thought I will wait here until they let him out; but he never came. It will be the same with your man. Go back to the village.'

Punchi Menika wept quietly from weariness and hunger and misery at the old man's words:

'It is no good crying,' he said; 'I am old, and who should know better than I? They never come out. It is better to go back to the village.'

Punchi Menika got up and walked slowly up the hill, and then round the prison. There was only one entrance to it, an immense solid wooden gate studded with iron nails. She knocked timidly, so timidly that the sound was not heard within. Then she sat down against the wall and waited. Hours passed, and nothing happened; the gate remained closed; no sound could be heard from within the prison; the hill was deserted except for the five cows whose coughing she could hear from time to time below her. But she waited patiently for something to happen, only moving now and again into the shadow of the wall, when the sun in its course beat down upon her.

At last the door opened, and a man in a khaki uniform and helmet, carrying a club in his hand, came out. He looked at Punchi Menika, and said sharply:

'What do you want here?'

'I have come about my man, aiya. A long time ago he was sent here for six months. The time has passed, but he has not returned to the village. They say he is dead. Is it true, aiya?'

'What was his name and village?'

'He was from Beddagama.'

'His name?'

'Aiya, how can I tell his name?'

'What was his name, fool?'

'They called him Babun.'

'What was he convicted for?'

'It was a false case. They said he had robbed the Arachchi.'

'Oh, that man, yes. The Arachchi was killed afterwards, wasn't he?'

'Yes, yes, my father did that.'

'Well, he was here, too. Have you any money, woman?'

'No, aiya, none; we are very poor.'

'Ah! well. We can't tell you anything here. You must go to Kamburupitiya, and send a petition to the Agent Hamadoru.'

'But you know my man, aiya; you said you did. What harm to tell me? Is he here now? What has happened to him? I have come many days' journey to ask about him, and now you send me away to more trouble.'

The jail guard looked at Punchi Menika for a minute or two.

'Well,' he said, 'charity they say is like rain to a parched crop. You are asking for drought in a parched field. I knew the man; he was here, but he is dead. He died two months back.'

The jail guard expected to hear the shrill cry and the beating of the breast, the signs of a woman's mourning. Punchi Menika astonished him by walking slowly away to the shade, and sitting down again by the prison wall. The blow was too heavy for the conventional signs of grief. She sat dry-eyed; she felt little, but the intense desire to get away to the village, to get away out of this world, where she was lost and alone, to the compound, where she could sit and watch the sun set behind the jungle. She did not wait long; she set out at once down the hill. The old man still sat among his cows looking at the cocoanut-trees.

'Ah,' he said, as she passed him, 'they never come out. I told you so.'

'He is dead, father.'

'Yes, they never come out. Go back to the village, child.'

'I am going, father.'

CHAPTER X

Two years later, Punchi Menika was still living in the hut which had belonged to Silindu, but she lived alone. Karlinahami had died slowly and almost painlessly, like the trees around her. Her death had brought no difference into Punchi Menika's life, except that now she had to find food for herself alone.

The years had brought more evil, death, and decay upon the village. Of the five houses which stood when Punchi Menika returned from her journey to the prison, only two remained, her own, and that of the headman Vederala Punchirala. Disease and hunger visited it year after year. It seemed, as the headman said, to have been forgotten by gods and men. Year after year, the rains from the north-east passed it by; only the sun beat down more pitilessly, and the wind roared over it across the jungle; the little patches of chena crop which the villagers tried to cultivate withered as soon as the young shoots showed above the ground. No man, traveller or headman or trader, ever came to the village now. No one troubled any longer to clear the track which led to it; the jungle covered it and cut the village off.

Disease and death took the old first, Podi Sinho, and his wife Angohami, and the jungle crept forward over their compound. And three years later two other huts were abandoned. In one had lived Balappu with his wife and sister, and his two children; in the other Bastian Appu with his two sons, a daughter, a daughter-in-law, and a grandchild. They had tried to help Punchi Menika by letting her work in their chenas, and by giving her a share in the meagre crop. They struggled hard against the fate that hung over them, clinging to the place where they had been born and lived, the compound they knew, and the sterile chenas which they had sown. No children were born to them now in their hut, there women were as sterile as the earth; the children that had been born to them died of want and fever. At last they yielded to the jungle. They packed up their few

possessions and left the village for ever, to try and find work and
food in the rice-fields of Maha Potana.

They tried to induce Punchi Menika to go with them, but she
refused. She remembered her misery and loneliness upon the
road to Tangalla, and the words of the old man from Mahawelagama, who sat among the cows upon the hill there. She
remembered Babun's words to the Mudalali, 'Surely it is a more
bitter thing to die in a strange place.' It might be a still bitterer
thing to live in a strange place. She was alone in the world; the
only thing left to her was the compound and the jungle which
she knew. She clung to it passionately, blindly. The love which she
had felt for Silindu and Babun – who were lost to her for ever,
whose very memories began to fade from her in the struggle to
keep alive – was transferred to the miserable hut, the bare
compound, and the parched jungle.

So she was left alone with Punchirala. He was an old man
now, weak and diseased. After a while he became too feeble even
to get enough food to keep himself alive. She took him into her
hut. She had to find food now for him, as well as for herself, by
searching the jungle for roots and fruit, and by sowing a few
handfuls of grain at the time of the rains in the ground about the
hut. He gave her no thanks; as his strength decayed, his
malignancy and the bitterness of his tongue increased; but he did
not live long after he came to her hut; hunger and age and
parangi at last freed her from his sneers and his gibes.

The jungle surged forward over and blotted out the village up
to the very walls of her hut. She no longer cleared the compound
or mended the fence, the jungle closed over them as it had closed
over the other huts and compounds, over the paths and tracks.
Its breath was hot and heavy in the hut itself which it imprisoned
in its wall, stretching away unbroken for miles. Everything
except the little hut with its rotting walls and broken tattered
roof had gone down before it. It closed with its shrubs and
bushes and trees, with the impenetrable disorder of its thorns
and its creepers, over the rice-fields and the tanks. Only a little
hollowing of the ground where the trees stood in water when
rain fell, and a long little mound which the rains washed out and

the elephants trampled down, marked the place where before
had lain the tank and its land.

The village was forgotten, it disappeared into the jungle from
which it had sprung, and with it she was cut off, forgotten. It
was as if she was the last person left in the world, a world of
unending trees above which the wind roared always and the sun
blazed. She became one of the beasts of the jungle, struggling
perpetually for life against hunger and thirst; the ruined hut,
through which the sun beat and the rains washed, was only the
lair to which she returned at night for shelter. Her memories of
the evils which had happened to her, even of Babun and her life
with him, became dim and faded. And as they faded, her
childhood and Silindu and his tales returned to her. She had
returned to the jungle; it had taken her back; she lived as she had
done, understanding it, loving it, fearing it. As he had said, one
has to live many years before one understands what the beasts
say in the jungle. She understood them now, she was one of
them. And they understood her, and were not afraid of her. They
became accustomed to the little tattered hut, and to the woman
who lived in it. The herd of wild pigs would go grunting and
rooting up to the very door, and the old sows would look up
unafraid and untroubled at the woman sitting within. Even the
does became accustomed to her soft step as she came and went
through the jungle, muttering greetings to them; they would
look up for a moment, and their great eyes would follow her for
a moment as she glided by, and then the heads would go down
again to graze without alarm.

But life is very short in the jungle. Punchi Menika was a very
old woman before she was forty. She no longer sowed grain, she
lived only on the roots and leaves that she gathered. The
perpetual hunger wasted her slowly, and when the rains came
she lay shivering with fever in the hut. At last the time came
when her strength failed her; she lay in the hut unable to drag
herself out to search for food. The fire in the corner that had
smouldered so long between the three great stones was out. In
the day the hot air eddied through the hut, hot with the breath of
the wind blowing over the vast parched jungle; at night she

shivered in the chill dew. She was ... ing, and the jungle knew it;
i ... t for death. When the end
v ... shadow glided into the
... her steadily, two immense
v ... t the darkness. She sat up,
f ... gle, blind agonising fear.
... med. 'He has come, the
... me as you said. Aiyo! save
n

a ... ed softly, and glided like

TWENTIETH-CENTURY CLASSICS

While more and more new novels of greater and lesser merit arrive on an already overcrowded literary scene, many fine ones from earlier decades are disappearing from booksellers' shelves. Beginning in October 1981, OUP will help to remedy the situation by regularly publishing in its Oxford Paperbacks series classic works of the twentieth century. Each will have a new introduction, a biographical note on the author, and a specially commissioned full-colour cover. Details of the first four Classics appear here. A further eight titles will be published next year, among them Adrian Bell's *Corduroy*, Rex Warner's *The Aerodrome*, and *The Secret Battle* by A. P. Herbert.

Elizabeth and Essex

Lytton Strachey

With a new introduction by Michael Holroyd

Lytton Strachey achieved fame with the publication in 1918 of *Eminent Victorians*, but it was his last book, *Elizabeth and Essex*, the story of the complex and stormy relationship between Queen Elizabeth I and the Earl of Essex, which brought him great popular success. The book was ahead of its time, both in its structure, derived by the author from the Elizabethan stage, and in the way in which its dialogue uses material culled from extant speeches and letters. It was to the 'new' theories of Dr Freud that Strachey looked to help him bring the main characters alive. Freud himself later read the book and commented that Strachey had 'probably succeeded in making a correct reconstruction of what actually occurred'. 'A brilliant and insufficiently appreciated book' – A. L. Rowse.

OXFORD PAPERBACKS

They were Defeated

Rose Macaulay

With a new introduction by Susan Howatch

They were Defeated, Rose Macaulay's only historical
novel, represents the flowering of her lifelong passion
for the seventeenth century. She loved the period for its
poets and thinkers, and was enthralled by the conflicting
ideals that finally brought Civil War. The book, which
in some ways foreshadows her final novel *The Towers
of Trebizond*, interweaves the lives of Robert Herrick
and other poets with those of a small group of fictional
characters. Their lives, and in particular the life of her
heroine Julian, are set vividly before us in a period that
was one of the most turbulent in English history. Susan
Howatch, author of the bestselling historical romances
Penmarric and *Cashelmara*, has written a new introduction explaining why, in the year of the centenary of Rose
Macaulay's birth, we should be reassessing her contri-
bution to twentieth-century literature. 'To the great
enrichment of the English language Miss Macaulay has
chosen an historical subject. As a result she has achieved
her greatest success' – *The Observer*.

The Rock Pool

Cyril Connolly

With a new introduction by Peter Quennell

A snobbish and mediocre young man from Oxford spends the summer in an artists' colony on the Riviera. Its members interest him. Fascinated but uninvolved, he observes them as he would creatures in a rock pool, until the denizens of the pool begin to drag him down into it ...

The Rock Pool, Connolly's only novel, brilliantly chronicles the clash of two cultures, but remains largely unknown even to readers familiar with his critical essays. An early work, it was first published in Paris in 1935, having been turned down by two London publishers on grounds of obscenity. It now appears as an Oxford Paperback in an unexpurgated version, prefaced by Connolly's original dedication to historian Peter Quennell in which he explains the difficulties he experienced in getting the book published, and with a new introduction by Quennell himself.

Vision and Design

Roger Fry

Edited with an introduction by J. B. Bullen,
Lecturer in English, University of Reading

'In so far as taste can be changed by one man, it was changed by Roger Fry', wrote Lord Clark of the man who was instrumental in introducing the modern French schools of painting to the British public, and who ardently championed Cézanne, Picasso, and Matisse in the face of hostility and derision. Roger Fry had an unprecedented influence on the artistic tastes of an entire generation, and the twenty essays on themes that occupied him throughout his life which are collected in this book make it one of the outstandingly important works of art criticism published during the present century. Those to whom the critical and art-historical background of the essays may be unfamiliar will find the introduction and notes provided for this edition very useful. Another feature is the addition of eight illustrations selected by the editor in collaboration with Roger Fry's daughter.

OXFORD PAPERBACKS

A. E. Housman:
The Scholar-Poet

Richard Perceval Graves

Since Housman's *A Shropshire Lad* was first published in 1896, it has never been out of print. Thousands of copies of the poems were carried by British soldiers into the trenches during the Great War; but few readers, then or since, have known anything of their author. This biography, which Geoffrey Grigson called 'able and civilized' when it first appeared in 1979, reveals Housman as a formidable classical scholar to whom poetry was merely a diversion, an agonized homosexual, and a lonely, melancholy man who was something of a mystery even to his friends. Based on detailed research, and incorporating a wealth of previously unpublished material, Richard Perceval Graves's book convincingly reconciles the apparently conflicting sides of Housman's personality, and reassesses his reputation. It now appears in paperback for the first time.

OXFORD PAPERBACKS

Moore: G. E. Moore and the Cambridge Apostles

Paul Levy

Leonard Woolf called him 'the only great man whom I have ever met in the world of ordinary, real life', Bertrand Russell was 'electrified' by him, and Virginia Woolf thought him 'a very great man'. In this book Paul Levy explains how G. E. Moore, a modest academic philosopher, came to have a considerable influence on English intellectual life. Moore was a leading figure of the Cambridge Apostles, a semi-secret university society devoted to the debate of philosophical questions, whose membership included Leonard Woolf, Bertrand Russell, Lytton Strachey and Roger Fry. The author's unrivalled access to G. E. Moore's personal papers, and those of the Apostles Society, enabled him to write this book, which was described as 'immensely enjoyable' by Mary Warnock in *The Listener* when it was first published in 1979. It now appears for the first time in paperback.